salvation today

ARNE SOVIK

FOREWORD BY
PHILIP POTTER

AUGSBURG PUBLISHING HOUSE
MINNEAPOLIS, MINNESOTA

SALVATION TODAY

Copyright © 1973 Augsburg Publishing House
Library of Congress Catalog Card No. 73-78252
International Standard Book No. 0-8066-1318-1

All rights reserved. No part of this book may be used or reproduced in any manner whatsoever without written permission except in the case of brief quotations in critical articles and reviews. For information address Augsburg Publishing House, 426 South Fifth Street, Minneapolis, Minnesota 55415.

Manufactured in the United States of America

Contents

Foreword by Philip Potter 5

Introduction 8

1. Salvation and the Missionary Movement 12

2. A World Redefining Itself 25

3. What Is Salvation? 44

4. Elements in Today's Mission: Proclaiming the
   New Life 57

5. Elements in Today's Mission:
   Improving the Common Life 74

6. An Affirmation of Salvation 87

Study Helps

   A. Twenty Questions 90

   B. Bible Study Suggestions 92

   C. For Further Reading 92

   D. Salvation Today:
      A Personal Statement by M. M. Thomas ... 93

   E. Salvation in Contemporary Experience:
      A Selection of Texts 102

Foreword

"Today salvation has come to this house" (Luke 19:9-10). This declaration of Christ to Zacchaeus has haunted me from my childhood. Perhaps psychologists might find this to be the clue to my obsession with the theme of "Salvation Today" for a world conference on mission—a theme which was at first (1967) considered unpopular and out of date by very respected and theologically sound missionary leaders. Perhaps a political analyst would explain my obsession by referring to the circumstances in which Jesus said these words to Zacchaeus—the latter's awakened social conscience which made him recognize the needs of the poor and also his unjust methods of acquiring wealth. After all, like over 50% of those who gathered at Bangkok, I come from the so-called Third World, those poor countries which have been the scene of modern missions and also of colonial and economic exploitation.

However, what captured my young mind and has grown on me with the years is the fact that Jesus, at a critical point in his ministry, took the risk of inviting himself to the home of this hated rich man who was an economic pirate, a traitor to his people who were struggling against Roman colonial rule. Above all, the face to face encounter with Christ had an explosive, radical and revolutionary effect on Zacchaeus. The impossible happened. A rich man was saved, liberated from himself and from all he stood for and did, and not only he but also those who were related to him, his house. In this experience of liberation, which was expressed in his action of justice and compassion, he recovered his identity as a son of Abraham, and therefore his community with his own people. He found himself and his people, in fact, all peoples.

It was this insight into the Gospel story which stimulated my colleagues and myself to organize this Conference on "Salvation Today." What conditioned the style and content of the meeting was our conviction that the gospel of the redeeming love of God in Christ in his death and resurrection has radical consequences for our whole existence, for the structures of our day-to-day relationships and for society. And this conviction was confirmed by the many activities in which we were involved in the Commission of World Mission and Evangelism since Mexico, 1963, and which were implicit since Edinburgh, 1910.

The real challenge of Bangkok is not in the contemporary concern for social ethics—social and racial justice, the issue of power whether of money, knowledge or personnel which has come to the fore in mission both at home and overseas. It is rather how we understand the salvation which Jesus brought into the world by his incarnation, ministry, and atonement. If we are not agreed on what the incarnation and the cross imply for Christian political action, it is because we have limited the scope and depth of God's action in Christ and therefore of the Christian mission. That is the challenge which Bangkok poses for us all—for our various theological and confessional positions, for our missionary policies and activities and, indeed, for our apprehension of God in his wonderful works in Christ and through his Holy Spirit in all who believe in him.

It is in this spirit that I heartily commend the story which Arne Sovik tells with such perceptiveness and out of a wealth of experience as a missionary and missionary statesman.

PHILIP A. POTTER

Introduction

This booklet is the result of a conference, but it is not a report on that conference.

It is rather a discussion of some of the issues raised and debated at the World Conference on Salvation Today, which was held in Bangkok, December 29, 1972 to January 8, 1973. The conference was called and organized by the Commission on World Mission and Evangelism of the World Council of Churches. It brought together some three hundred participants from sixty-nine countries, most of them chosen by the Christian councils of those countries.

Bangkok was the eighth in an influential series of missionary conferences that began with the Edinburgh Missionary Conference in 1910 and included Jerusalem in 1928, Madras in 1938, and others in the post-war era not so well-known.

The previous conference of the series, Mexico City, 1963, had raised a question for consideration: "What is the form and content of the salvation which Christ offers to men and women in the secular world?" The theme of Bangkok was derived from this question. It turned out to be a theme that excited lively, sometimes impassioned, discussion throughout the world during preparations for Bangkok. As more than one critic has pointed out, the Conference brought no final massive consensus. There could hardly be, for the delegates and the invited consultants had all been chosen with a view to bring to the conference the whole broad spectrum of Christian missionary thought. If the pages following do not betray a certain inconsistency and disagreement, they will not be true to the facts of the present Christian understanding of salvation, or to the debate at Bangkok. Yet, for all its disagreements, the Conference will certainly be seen as a significant way station in the neverending process of thinking about the message and mission of the Christian church.

The Conference itself would be worth some attention. Its style and content made it a new experience, even—perhaps especially—for old conference-goers. There was an emphasis on corporate work rather than individual performance. There was insistent pressure to keep the discussions in context. What is the world today? How does it apprehend life? How does the church minister? To get answers we had "action reports" from all over the world. Participation in Bangkok was meant to be a series of encounters rather than of study sessions; and to a considerable extent this intention was met. The key word was *apprehend* rather than *comprehend*. We felt and saw and acted—and thought. In short, Bangkok was a "happening."

One inevitable consequence of this kind of conference was the relatively limited number of documented results at the end of the meeting. The 1938 Madras Conference produced one major theological work and a seven-volume conference report that is still a standard reference work in the study of missions. Bangkok will have less to say on paper. A collection of preparatory articles and papers written over the last four years by groups and individuals working on the theme would fill a considerable volume. Post-conference commentary may be equally voluminous. The official documents (addresses, reports, and some preparatory studies) will be included in the published Report of the Conference. But the major effort at spreading the word about Salvation Today will be carried out in the constituencies themselves. The sponsors have encouraged national or regional organizations to prepare their own interpretive materials for their own people. In North America the National Council of the Churches of Christ in the U.S.A. is undertaking a major effort in audiovisual materials on Salvation Today, including tapes and films from Bangkok.

This study volume is another instrument for the North American constituency, including the United States and Canada. It is an attempt to gather and discuss in brief compass those issues which were dealt with in Bangkok and in the whole study process. It is meant to be used for individual study or in study groups, and to that end resource materials are found after Chapter 6. They include study questions, suggestions for Bible study and for further reading, and perhaps most important, the seminal paper presented at Bangkok by Dr. M. M. Thomas of India.

Many readers will feel that questions related to the healing of society are over-emphasized. Admitted. The discussion today happens to be concentrated on social ethics, and not on the doctrine of the atonement. In Bangkok at least there seemed to be very general agreement from one end of the church to the other that the world is redeemed through the Savior who is Son of God and Son of Man. The agreement was not so universal on what the incarnation and the cross implied for Christian action in public affairs.

Every reader will find something missing in this booklet, something important to the discussion. I'm sorry; it's a small book. I am grateful to the people who have been helpful in its writing. To name them might be to implicate them in the shortcomings for which I am responsible. One name must be mentioned: my wife Ruth edited and typed the manuscript. The Adult Forum of First Lutheran Church, Montclair, New Jersey, has been the unseen audience for whom I have written. If its members and others of God's people can through these pages be helped to minister a little more faithfully, compassionately, and effectively to a world in need of salvation, the writer's purpose will have been served.

1.

Salvation and the Missionary Movement

Salvation today? God knows we need it! The streets are not safe at night. Our savings go down the drain of inflation, and the price of everything never stops going up. Who knows if there will even be a job tomorrow? Our leaders can't hold things together, and the nation is a house divided against itself. The struggle of the poor and the minorities for their rights never seems to end, and people don't seem to care. Life seems to be too long for some of the aged, and the younger generation doesn't like the world they were brought into. Everything that seemed so certain a few years ago has suddenly gone soft. What is to be depended on? Salvation?

God knows where we would be if we didn't have that hope. But is that salvation today?

The purpose of this book is to say something about that question. It is to probe into what the Christian church is about when it talks to the whole world about the man who came to a corrupt tax collector named Zacchaeus and said, "Today salvation has come to your house." We are going to have to begin by looking at the meaning of the word salvation in history, and we shall discover that it has not always meant the same thing.

Jesus and Salvation

Something happened to the followers of Jesus. He called it, and they called it, and we call it *salvation*. It had been fore-shadowed in the Old Testament records of the Jewish people. It was bound up with the stories of Adam and Eve and Noah, with Abraham's leaving home and becoming a prosperous nomadic herdsman, with the deliverance from Egypt and entry into the promised land, with the prosperity of a monotheistic people, with Israel's decline and fall, with the return from Babylon, with life as a Jewish nation even in exile and under foreign rulers. But it was more than a corporate, national experience of God's care. It was the personal, vivid experience of God's protection and support and leading that Moses had, and David and the prophets and countless unrecorded others, and it came to include the hope of life after death and a new world.

But when Jesus came, it took on a meaning that it had never had before. Here was suddenly a changed life, charged with power, free for anyone who wanted it. The lame could walk, the sinner somehow repent and leave his ways, the bigot find release, the hopeless find a future and fearful boldness. The disciples were overwhelmed by this Jesus whose teaching molded them, whose death and resurrection brought them first to despair and then to the joy of life renewed. They drew the only possible conclusion—here was the Messiah, the promised one of God, God himself incarnate.

Here was salvation indeed! The book of Acts tells the story of the inevitable consequences of the disciples' experience with Jesus, of their efforts to explain it, and of the beginnings of a religious institution that enabled them to preserve, practice, and propagate the good news of what was happening—for it continued to happen, this change called salvation. The epistles began the long and still continuing documentation of Christians' attempts to explain, both to their own satisfaction and for others, who precisely Jesus was, what his coming had meant and would mean.

For Christian theology is nothing more than the attempt to explain the event of Jesus Christ, its origins and consequences. And this theological process went on within the corporate life of believers living in cultures that resulted from the dialogic interaction of the church's convictions about Jesus with the values and ideas of the times. From its understanding of the revelation, tempered by its own needs, its own conditions, the early church derived its message of salvation to the world in which it lived. It was a vital enough message, and uniquely enough lived, so that—in spite of periodic persecutions and in spite of its humble origins—the church grew. And only three hundred years after Christ, in a burst of expansion that sharply diluted the quality of the community, the church became the dominant religious institution in the vast Roman empire.

Salvation in the Middle Ages

With the establishment by the Emperor Constantine of Christianity as the state religion, a new era began. "Salvation" was now imposed on the population by decree, and the church became so identified with the culture that its cutting edge—in thought, in teaching, and in practice—came to be embodied largely in the monastic communities of Christians who lived in a paradoxical relationship of rejection of and service to the wider society of Christendom.

These communities, corrupt as they may sometimes have been, were nevertheless the means through which, after the fall of Rome, the life and the institutions of Christianity spread. Through them the notions of salvation of those lawless and barbaric, yet romantic centuries of the Dark and the Middle Ages in Europe were formed. Given the static and cruelly class-conscious feudal society, we can scarcely wonder at the fact that salvation was generally thought of as escape from the evils of the world and from punishment for sin. When one cannot change things, one's hopes naturally rest on the future.

The best monks and nuns brought with them wherever they went a certain limited scholarship, some small improvements in farming methods, and examples of compassion; but their major message was that the church was the ark of salvation. Through it heaven, the best hope of the people, could be attained; through it hell, their greatest fear, could be avoided. The churches of medieval Europe that towered over the village roofs, more magnificent, more elegant by far than the noble's castle, show that the church was also the sacred center of corporate life; it blessed and was blessed, it was loved as it was feared. It was the last refuge, but it was also apart from and critical of the transitory nature of all the triumphs and defeats of the battle of life. There is nothing in the North American architectural scene that so eloquently symbolizes the dominant value of the eternal over the temporal as do the centuries-old churches and cathedrals dominating the villages and towns of Europe. Salvation was hope for the future and solace for the present.

Yet, had the center of Christian life and witness not fled from the congregation to the monastery, had the church not succumbed to the charms of other-worldliness, would the history of post-Roman Europe have been less dark, less full of the contrast of saint and sinner? And more able to reach out east and south? Was the otherworldliness of salvation perhaps a cause as much as a result of the Middle Ages?

Early in the life of the church the theologians borrowed Greek metaphysical categories and separated the soul from the body. The latter was given only passing value, and the "salvation of the soul" was the pearl of great price. The result was two distortions. One was the subordination of the body which in consequence diverted theology from concern with the daily round. Healing, for example, an obvious gift to the New Testament church, was soon secularized, and the science of medicine lost all connection with theology.

The other distortion was the focus of faith upon the saving of the soul, which encouraged people to conceive of religion as a complex device to escape the threats of eternal punishment rather than a celebration of God's creative and liberating presence in human life. Immediately related to this understanding was the placing of happiness in the present world and eternal salvation in opposition to each other. One's life was lived in tension between the pleasures of the now and those of the hereafter. And the name of the game was to extract what one could from the present without throwing away all hope for the future. If, by devices such as indulgences, one could cheat the hangman, that was a legitimate ploy in the salvation transaction. Salvation was scarcely a joyful thing, and God was the enemy of everyday happiness. Young Luther was not unique in his disparagement of the body. Nor is this view of salvation unknown today. You pay your money and you take your choice—soul or body—now or later. Salvation by these lights is as much a threat as a promise.

Renaissance and Reformation

The Renaissance, that remarkable burst of energy and flowering of inventiveness that introduced the modern world, gave a new sense of potential to human life. The springs from which Renaissance man drank were only in part biblical. He drew on the rediscovered knowledge of the ancient world and on contacts with the vital Muslim culture as well. And salvation was on its way to another redefinition.

For that section of Europe that became Protestant the redefinition came earliest. It accompanied a breakdown of feudalism and the vision of a reformed society. In Germany the radical Christian Thomas Münzer died in 1525 attempting to establish by force a theocratic state, with both democratic and communistic ideas. He was one of many who drew far-reaching social consequences from the gospel. Calvin in Geneva was less radical and more successful. Salvation to him implied, besides heaven, a certain righteous, orderly, and prosperous society, and this kind of society, made up of righteous, upright, and prosperous individuals on earth, was a token of God's promise to be fulfilled in the future. Furthermore, a blessed society like that was worth defending by the sword, and a tyrant whose rule prevented true worship by the righteous believing community could and should in obedience to God be rebelled against. Salvation began to find roots in this life, in the social order. And a few decades later the Puritans brought this Calvinist tradition to American soil.

The Missionary Movement

The expansion of the church out of its traditional homeland in Europe began with those curious examples of missionary zeal, the Spanish and Portuguese explorers and *conquistadores*, who changed the map of the world in the decades following Columbus' epic voyage. As they set up their colonies in the far corners of Latin America, they combined an utter disregard for the welfare of the conquered peoples with a determination to save the souls of those they enslaved or murdered. Pizarro in Peru forced the Inca to accept baptism on threat of his life, and then had him murdered before he could apostatize. But Bartolomeo de las Casas and Pedro Claver were but the best known of the many monks who, within the limits of the vision of their time, tried to ameliorate the tyranny and oppression exercised by empire and church alike on the confused and decimated peoples of Latin America.

It is in Latin America that the heritage of the Middle Ages has persevered the longest, with its elements of feudalism, superstition, and other-worldliness, vast contrasts of poverty and wealth, and withal a sort of Christendom. For the historian and anthropologist Latin America has offered for study the last islands remaining of living but late medieval Christendom.

Sixteenth century missions in India were different only in that the political power of the Iberians was less overwhelming. The view of salvation was the same. Down the Malabar coast St. Francis Xavier is said to have led his little band of evangelists from one fishing village to the next, ringing a bell to call the people together, preaching briefly, baptising and then moving on in passionate devotion to the task of saving the greatest number of souls possible from destruction. Today the visitor on a drive down the coast passes a chain of white-washed Iberian-style village churches, mute witnesses to the enduring power of that kind of mass evangelism. But after four hundred years of Christian presence, the Christian fishermen are scarcely distinguishable from their Hindu or Muslim neighbors in life and customs, and they earn their precarious livelihood on the sea in a way that would have presented no surprises to St. Francis—except for, in the last decade, the nylon nets!

There had been from the very beginning of the missionary movement in the sixteenth century an ambiguity in the relationship of that movement to the commercial and government interests of European colonialists. In the nineteenth century, as colonialism crested, the cause of this ambiguity became clearer. The largely unexamined identification of salvation with the missionaries' own western cultural environment came out into the open.

The Portuguese and Spanish concordats with Rome in the sixteenth century provided among other things for state support for the missions that sprang up in the New World and elsewhere. To this day the Catholic missions in Portugese African colonies are supported by the colonial government and are regarded as agents of government policy. "Portugese Catholic missions," reads an agreement between the Vatican and Portugal dated as late as 1940, "are considered to be of imperial usefulness; they have an eminently civilizing influence." All bishops and superiors are to be Portugese and will have the right to salary and pension from the government at an appropriate level: "bishops and governors will all have the same salary." "Missionary congregations . . . will be financed according to need by the government," which will also "continue to make free grants of land to Catholic missions" (IDOC Documentation Project. "The Future of the Missionary Enterprise." No. 1, Jan. 1973, p. 12).

In the eighteenth century, the Protestant colonial forces of Western Europe were by no means sure that they wanted missionaries. Ziegenbalg, who sailed for India in 1706 with the support of Frederick IV of Denmark, spent months in Tranquebar as guest of the colony's governor—in jail. William Carey, a century later, could find no foothold in the territories of the British East India Company and had to settle in the Danish colony of Serampore. The Company, which provided chaplains for its own personnel, had no intention of allowing its relations with the Indians to be disturbed by the gospel. In the Carribbean, the Moravians who came to minister to the slaves were generally not welcomed by the planters and often suffered with their people.

In Pennsylvania in the same period the Quakers and Moravian missionaries to the Indians were constantly at odds with the colonists, whose interests were not served by living with the Indians but by moving them out. The invidious position of the missionary, suspected by the Indian because he was white and a purveyor of change—and no doubt also because of his sense of superiority—and despised by the settlers as a soft-headed do-gooder, was not unlike many among us today who try to build cultural and religious bridges.

In China in the nineteenth century, foreign powers had come to see themselves as protectors not only of their national commercial interests but also of all Christian missions, and maintained not only by diplomatic but also military means a protecting hand over both foreigners and Chinese Christians. The special status of Christians in China, which made them practically invulnerable to Chinese law, led as might be expected to all kinds of abuses. In the law courts Christians, if they could claim persecution, could win almost any case. The application of these special privileges varied; yet, because it limited and derogated the sovereignty of the Chinese government over its own citizens as well as resident foreigners and in effect made Chinese Christians into Westerners, it occasioned bitter resentment against Christianity. In 1943, after years of increasingly rare appeals to the unequal and unjust laws of "extraterritoriality," they were abolished. One wonders today how China missionaries of the nineteenth century could accept, not to say plead for, the political support of foreign and colonial governments. The answer lies in the history of Christianity in China.

Christianity had been banned in the early eighteenth century in China. The reason had little to do with convictions about eternal salvation; the sophisticated Confucian tradition could tolerate a good deal of latitude in popular religious belief and practice. But the irony was that the other-worldly faith the Jesuits had brought to the Peking court was seen to be a threat to the this-worldly order of the Empire. It brought novel ideas that threatened the age-old system; it brought links and loyalties with seafaring nations that threatened with their guns the very coasts of the Empire. Behind this "bamboo curtain" lived the most populous nation on earth. To reach it with the word of salvation it seemed entirely proper to the missionaries of the nineteenth century to ally themselves with the Christian powers of the West as the only means of opening China to the gospel. The Chinese state was, to their minds, both heathen and corrupt in any case.

Salvation and Western Civilization

By the middle of the nineteenth century as European expansionism approached its height, the pattern of modern missionary activity had assumed forms which betrayed certain general convictions about salvation, the content of the Christian mission. It was by this time thoroughly identified with western civilization and antagonistic to the cultures of Asia and Africa. The China missionaries wore Chinese garb to avoid public attention, not because they were admirers of it. Alexander

Duff declared that the missionaries' intent was not to improve the Hindu way of life but to "blow it to pieces." And David Livingstone went to Africa, as he said, to bring "the gospel and the blessings of European civilization."

The nature of any religious change, however otherworldly in dogma the new faith may be, is to effect cultural and social change in this world. If this was true in the essentially static culture of the medieval church, it was doubly so in the nineteenth century. The traditional societies of Asia and Africa were under attack by an increasingly aggressive West in politics, economics, and cultural influence. The tide of change by which we are now overwhelmed was then rising. Progress was an article of faith. A partner in the Western penetration, the churches, particularly the Protestants, brought more than an other-worldly word of salvation clothed in Western thought patterns of these traditional societies. Influenced not only by the Renaissance and the Reformation but also by Wesley and the continental pietists the missionary movement brought, wherever it went three institutions: the congregation, the school, and the hospital. Less self-consciously it also brought with it a tacit or explicit attack on the traditional social structure, and the promotion of individualism, support for capitalism and the market economy, and the exaltation of the Western way of life, which was almost always supported by a crass racism and lack of comprehension of the local religious and social values.

One should not be unduly critical. Any movement is a child of its times; the missionaries were vastly more sensitive and sympathetic to the cultures and the peoples they found than the political and commercial interests of the West, and they were often at odds with these interests. As a Caribbean bishop pointed out in Bangkok, the missionaries did introduce education, did suffer both for and with the slaves, did work for emancipation, and did help the people not only to endure the present but also to prepare for the future. Almost all anti-colonial independence movements have drawn major leadership from the churches, and most of the heads of the new African states are products of Christian schools.

Whatever the shortcomings of the missionary movement of the nineteenth century, the church spread and grew more rapidly, and in a manner unlike anything that had happened before. The expansion was by no means regular, planned, or consistent. By the time, for example, that missions began in New Guinea eighty-five years ago, some islands of the South Pacific had already become Christian, and their churches sent missionaries who worked side by side with Europeans. In South India the church grew almost explosively among the lowest classes, the outcastes—to whom Christianity offered, quite apart from hope of heaven, a new chance on earth to escape from an inhuman social system. Here was salvation of a very specific kind! Here whole families and villages and tribes came to the faith in a pattern that most missionaries wished for, but few worked systematically to attain. Sometimes—and this was especially true in the more sophisticated cultures or classes of society—people were persuaded slowly, one by one, and baptism meant expulsion from society and sometimes death.

It is common to think of "missions" as flowing from Europe and North America to Asia and Africa. In fact one must not forget that from colonial times up to the present day the successive waves of ethnic immigration to North and South America have been accompanied by missionaries sent from the European homelands, without whom the New World might well have lapsed into paganism. Wesley began as a young missionary in

Georgia. The same German society that sent missionaries to the tribes of Sumatra and South Africa also sent missionaries to the German immigrants in North and South America. Salvation was, in a way, the preservation of European Christian life and culture in a strange land! In North America, too, the heritage of a missionary movement which identified salvation with a Western European way of life is evident.

Thus with the changing centuries the Christian understanding of salvation has been shaped and reshaped. It has always been grounded in the revelation of Scripture, to be sure, but it has been modified by the changing character of the culture in which the church has lived and proclaimed the message, and expressed in terms of what its messengers have seen to be the needs of men. Jesus Christ is indeed the same yesterday, today and forever. But his salvation is new every morning. John Keble, the hymn writer, exulted in that daily newness:

> New every morning is the love
> Our wakening and uprising prove ...
> New perils past, new sins forgiven,
> New thoughts of God, new hopes of heaven.

2.

A World Redefining Itself

By the middle of the twentieth century Christianity seemed to have reached the height of its influence. Missionaries were to be found around the globe in unprecedented numbers. The Bible in part or whole had appeared in 2000 languages. Church membership in North America was at the highest point in history, and members supported the churches' work as never before. The proliferation of denominations, so much decried, was of course a symptom of selfishness and obduracy. But it was also an inevitable result of our multi-national background and our pluralistic society, and a mark of bursting vitality in the churches.

The Reformation had brought to Christianity a renewal of concern for this world, and the centuries since then had seen that concern grow. The church in mission in this century was encouraged by the nineteenth century's faith in progress, and by its actions helped to increase that faith. It identified with the dominant culture, but it also criticized it. It grew in effective participation in public affairs, but much too late to forestall the rise of another faith with a completely this-worldly orientation—Marxism. Age-old habits of racism were uncovered for what they were. The public and the churches, especially the "peace churches," supported the struggle for world peace and aid for the world's poor, and governments worked together in a constantly expanding conglomeration of international agencies.

Yet for every triumphal note raised, we could also see in our indifferent and selfish society evidence of religious weakness, retrogression, and decline. As Gibbon traced the roots of the decline of the Roman Empire back to centuries before its full flower, so some could see in the prosperous church of our day marks of decay. The growing feeling of *malaise* attacked particularly the Roman Catholic and Protestant establishments. By the 1960s some were asking not only if we were now at the end of the great period of missionary expansion that had begun with the nineteenth century but if we were entering a "post-Christian age" at home. The phrase "loss of nerve" appeared in troubled conversations. Statisticians began to predict that the proportion of Christians in the world was beginning to decline; indeed one projection forecast that in the next generation Christians would drop from 30% to 20% of the world's population. This calculation was, it would seem now, rather farfetched; it was more an indication of the rejection of "triumphalism" and of resignation than anything else. But bright dreams of a world turned Christian seemed to have gone sour, and somehow the vivid life and rapid growth of Christianity in some other continents did not seem to compensate for the apparent secularization of Europe and North America. Introspection and self-criticism became almost fashionable.

The End of Missions?

What has made the church doubt its calling as the instrument of God for men's salvation? One cannot here go deeply into the reasons for this disquiet—the philosophical reasons with roots in the Enlightenment, and the political, sociological, psychological reasons that have joined the attacks of secular scientism and Marxism upon all religion. But one can note some of the more obvious symptoms of this spirit of doubt as it expresses itself in relation to the Christian missionary movement.

Most critically, there are those who doubt the uniqueness of the Christian revelation. Was not Mangu Khan, the Mongol Emperor, right when he said to Friar William, "Like the five fingers of the hand, so are the several ways to paradise"? The increasing knowledge we have of the values found in other faiths, and our increasing awareness of the incompleteness of our apprehension of the truth expressed in the Christianity we practice and teach (1 Cor. 13:12 and 2 Cor. 4:7), have raised questions about is uniqueness and absoluteness. Does God perhaps move outside the church? The rational argument against particularity, (against God's revealing himself to man in one specific way, in one place, and at one time through one Person) gains strength when the circumstantial evidence for this particularity, moral and cultural superiority, is hard to demonstrate.

In *Ecumenicity and Evangelism* (Eerdmans: Grand Rapids, 1970, p. 50) David A. Stowe has analyzed the opposition of Reinhold Niebuhr to missions to the Jews. He notes that one ground for this opposition is Niebuhr's belief that theologically Judaism and Christianity are so close that conversion from one faith to the other makes no sense. Projecting the argument to apply to other faiths, Dr. Stowe concludes quite validly that Niebuhr's position is ultimately a subtle rejection of all missions, for a sympathetic valuation of any religion will discern many elements of truth and value systems not inferior to those of acculturated Christendom.

When in New Delhi at the 1961 Assembly of the World Council of Churches, Joseph Sittler, a Lutheran theologian, spoke of the "cosmic Christ," a Christ whose presence pervades the universe and who is already there when the Christian witness comes to proclaim his salvation, he not only stated a profound biblical truth (ch. Eph. 1:20-21); he also legitimized a feeling that many had long entertained—that God's redemption is not reserved for those who know and explicitly accept the historical biblical revelation and become members of the institutional church. From here it is a short, if illogical, leap for some to the conclusion that there is no need for missions.

There are others who raise questions about the superiority of the Christian witness and the Christian ethic. The complacent nineteenth century attitude toward the "enlightened" Christian world and its burden for the reputedly corrupt and backward cultures of Asia and Africa has given way to a far more self-critical attitude as we have seen the fruits of two world wars, of expansionist greed, of racism and nationalism in what was once Christendom. What evidence is there for the ethical superiority of Christianity as a social force? President Radhakrishnan of India is said to have told a group of Christians, "You Christians seem to us like a lot of very ordinary people making some extraordinary claims." The Christians responded quite properly, "We make no claim for ourselves. Our claims are for Christ our Lord." To which the Hindu philosopher gave the devastating answer, "Why should I expect Christ to do more for me than he seems to have done for you?" (Stowe, p. 39). Most recent visitors to China have found there a society which in contrast to the often chaotic and problem-ridden nations of the West seems orderly, relatively just, and in comparison with the old China very effective in solving its problems. Yet its theoretical base is humanist and materialist.

The demand that a religious faith validate itself in the lives of its followers is reasonable. Sensitivity to this point has led some Christians in recent months to question whether it would be proper for American Christians, now that the military withdrawal from Vietnam has taken place, to begin evangelistic work there. Must we not, they ask, first establish some sort of credibility by pouring our efforts into relief and rehabilitation? Have we any right to preach in Vietnam? But this is an attempt to justify ourselves by our virtues, unconsciously seeing ourselves as superior to those to whom we preach, living by works rather than grace. The Christian evangelist dare not base his work on anything but a desire to share the grace of God which he has come to know. But the hearer has every right to expect that knowledge of God's grace should not be without its fruits in human relations and in the social order. (See Section E in the *Study Helps*.)

Still others doubt the church's calling as an instrument of men's salvation because of a bad conscience. It may be called the "you-can't-preach-to-a-starving-man" syndrome. It is, of course, sound Christianity that when a person is hungry the thing to do is to feed him. And the ministry of the affluent middle class churches—whether at home or overseas—includes concern both for charity and for justice in regard to the physical needs of men. But our uneasy consciences about our failure to share, and about our indirect or direct participation in the exploitation of the poor of this world, must not so cripple us with remorse that the right of the world to hear the gospel is forgotten.

At what point is it legitimate to be concerned for the

whole man and not just the body? At what point does the priority for development yield to priority for the proclamation of Christ? What is the "minimum standard" below which people are supposed to be impervious to the word of grace? Is it to be set by the statistician in Washington or the villager in Africa? Is there any evidence to show that having reached a given standard of living a man's hunger for bread will end and he will be prepared for spiritual things? In truth, man cannot be so separated into component parts, and if concern for the spirit without concern for the body is sterile, the converse is also true.

There is a considerable embarrassment among thoughtful Christians over the link between colonialism (including white expansion in North America) and the missionary movement. "When the white men first came they had the Bibles and we the land," a Pacific islander is supposed to have said. "Now we have the Bibles and the white man has the land." To the orthodox Marxist, missions are seen as an integral aspect of capitalist imperialism; hence the resistance of Eastern European governments to the very term "missions" and the sharp insistence of the Chinese People's Republic that the churches in China break all ties with their overseas supporters.

Quite apart from ideological theories which ignore some obvious facts in history, the long and complex relationship of mutual support, interdependence, use of each other, and tension between colonialism and missions cannot be denied. Even if today political colonialism is all but gone, the much more complex cultural and economic aspects of Western imperialism still concern us; and because Christian missions have inevitably their deep cultural and economic consequences, many have conscientious questions about their impact.

The spokesman for missions will point out that all the external influences that have disturbed the non-Western world in the last centuries, the missionary movement has been the only one that has had as its basic motivation an honest concern for the peoples of that part of the world. He will add that if the churches have been related to colonialism they must be seen as ameliorative, agents of disruption to be sure, but agents of service rather than of exploitation. Yet the problem is not easily brushed off; it was struggled with throughout the Bangkok Conference.

A final internal reason for Christians' doubts has come with the increasing knowledge of cultural anthropology and the difficulties of cross-cultural communication. To convey clearly the message of a gracious God acting in the cross of Christ is not easy in the most favorable of circumstances, where language and cultural values are shared. The minister who extends an invitation to church membership surely is issuing that as an invitation to join a community of sinners, to be a guest at God's table, to use Jesus' figure. But is not that invitation often accepted as an invitation to join an organization devoted to the promotion of morality and order, membership in which is a mark of respectability? A Swiss pastor poet describes the way of salvation that has developed in that orderly society:

> This is an upright country
> with clean people
> and with clean salvation systems
> which are all on "go."
>
> After his birth
> every citizen
> still squirming
> is laid on the assembly line
> and automatically

machined by ceremonies
until the last one
lovingly ejects him
into the Elysian fields

This is an upright country
with clean people
and with clean salvation systems
which are all on "go."

> Kurt Marti
> *Gedichte am Rand*
> Verlag Arthur Niggli
> Translation by Thomas Wieser

But how shall the church then communicate the gospel to those of culture and language not informed by the biblical tradition, to Chinese, for example, where the closest possible Chinese word to *sin* may bear the connotation of suffering rather than guilt? Or to Eskimos, who have no idea what a lamb might be, or to Japanese, where the father figure is counted one of the three traditional disasters? Missionaries have seldom required that people learn English before they become Christians, but they have often required almost as thorough a cultural change. And indeed some of the rigid "salvation systems" that are brought from the West are so unintelligible in another culture that one may properly ask if in fact the Christianity that is heard and accepted is the same faith as that which was preached.

The fact that faith is faith in the One rather than acceptance of some system of doctrine alone makes the transmission of the faith possible. For all of the expressions and understandings of the faith are culturally conditioned. A missionary in New Guinea preaches in what he considers a simple and clear manner. He uses certain forms of prayer. The hearer is overwhelmed by one outstanding fact, that the white man has "cargo," goods which come to him in ships from over the horizon or drop out of the distant sky in great winged creatures. How can he get some too? And because his whole world is one of mystery and ritual, he attempts by imitation of the missionary's words and ways to bring the cargo. Thus originate the cargo cults of Melanesia.

One need not go so far afield to find other examples of the disjunction between what is preached and what is heard and received. The Gothic Age built churches and lavished on them the skill and genius of the anonymous artists of the people. The modern esthete is attracted to them, and to a medieval kind of Christianity because he finds in them expressions of human creativity. The missionary teaches the outcaste Indian peasant of heaven, but the Indian is converted because he finds in the church an opening to a new dignity and humanness in this life, not the next. The church operates school systems to make its children literate Christians; they study in them because these schools are the gateway to modern living.

And yet the greatest reason for the need to reconsider our Christian role as God's instruments of salvation lies in none of the doubts and fears that have beset the churches. It lies in the ferment of change around us that has occasioned these doubts and fears which compel us to question all the assumptions that have until now been taken for granted. The times we live in require us to rethink our message and our mission. "Salvation Isn't the Same Today" reads the headline over one report on Bangkok. More radically, a writer of one of the pre-conference studies declares that "saving my soul does not interest me as a man in 1972" (George Johnston in IRM, Jan. 1972, p. 48). Still more radically the historian Hannah Arendt describes ours as an age "where man, wherever he goes, encounters only himself."

The Context of Mission

What is this world like, this world that is the context of the Christian proclamation of salvation? Philip Potter, General Secretary of the World Council of Churches, in his report to Bangkok analyzed today's world by pointing out three paradoxes. Much of the material in the remainder of this chapter, including such quotations as are not otherwise credited, are drawn from Dr. Potter's report to the Bangkok Conference.

The first paradox is that a world that is unified by technology is nevertheless desperately divided by the human factors of politics, economics and race.

> We are now living at an accelerated pace, in one world in which all peoples are drawn together through science and technology, rapid means of communications and the mass media. Indeed, the great new fact of our time is the coming into modern world history of millions of hitherto submerged peoples who belong to those areas which have hitherto been called mission lands—Asia, the Pacific islands, Africa, Latin America and the Caribbean. The news of the world can be heard in every land and can be seen on the television screen while it is happening.

One is reminded of the Sunday school lessons about the "fulness of time" that marked the first coming of Jesus, the *pax Romana* that prepared the way for the initial spread of Christianity. How much more favorable, from the point of view of externals, are the conditions today for a message "to the nations"! No wonder, as Dr. Potter continued, "the fact of one world has held out great prospects for the world mission of the church. The eschatological words of Christ have become very vivid and urgent: "This gospel of the Kingdom will be preached throughout the whole world (*oikumene*), as a testimony to the nations" (Matt. 24:14). Is this not the day when, if ever, we should be speaking of "the evangelization of the world in this generation"?

But the unity offered by technological advance and the worldwide flow of information and ideas and by the structures of world organization is only one side of the coin. This same world is split by the bitter political rivalries of the major powers with their ideological antagonisms and their fears and ambitions. It is divided too into Koreas and Vietnams and Sudans and Burundis, whose bitter civil struggles are too often subsidiary to the conflicts of the big powers.

These conflicts are related to economic realities. The superior technological capacities of the great powers have been constantly employed against the poorer peoples. This is a fact that is as real as the exploitation of the poor by the wealthy on our continent, where, a recent study shows, the gap between rich and poor has been widening in spite of such governmental controls as we have.

The decade of the sixties was touted throughout the world as the Decade of Development. Churches at all levels of organization joined other voluntary and governmental agencies, and great efforts were made to change the situation. There have been some happy results, but on the whole even such massive efforts could not overcome basic inequalities in the world economic system. The poorer nations are now at a greater disadvantage than ever. President Allende of Chile summed it up at the 1972 meeting of the UN Conference on Trade and Development in Santiago:

> Over the past twenty years, the flow of foreign capital into the Third World has meant a net loss for us of many hundreds of millions of dollars, besides leaving us in debt to the tune of nearly

seventy thousand millions. If to this debt we add our real, although invisible, losses resulting from the decline in the prices of our exports and the increase in the cost of everything we import, it can clearly be seen that since the war international economic relations have caused a damage to the peripheral countries of over one hundred thousand million dollars.

Direct investment of foreign capital, often presented as an instrument for progress, has almost always proved harmful. For example, between 1950 and 1967, according to data furnished by the Organization of American States, Latin America received $3,900,000,000 and disbursed $20,800,000,000. In other words, our region paid out four dollars for every dollar it received.

It comes as no surprise when the economist Charles Elliott declares that "international disparities in wealth represent the greatest human and therefore Christian moral problem of this century" [*The Development Debate* (London: SCM Press, 1971), p. 12].

The Christian mission has always been concerned with justice and human welfare. The early church and the medieval monks laid the foundations for a richer and broader economic and social life

> ... through their proclamation of the gospel of man's liberation from the forces of nature and the fear of each other. This tradition has been wonderfully carried forward in the past two hundred years or so by the modern missionary movement from Europe and North America to the rest of the world, through the preaching and teaching of the gospel, through education, medical care, agricultural and social work. And yet the facts of the past decade

show the continuing appalling exploitation by the rich nations of the poorer nations, even in the name of development. Development has been seen purely in economic terms and that means on the basis of the structures, values and dynamics of societies which adhere to the doctrine of the survival of the fittest. A closer look at the situation shows clearly that the rich nations are spiritually and morally underdeveloped, functioning on the philosophy of aggressive individual and corporate egoism. Development, like mission, must be seen to involve six continents.

A third and particularly divisive force in this time of technological unity is racism and particularly white racism. The imperialist expansion of the Western nations in the last centuries was marked by an overweening sense of white racial superiority, and the missionary movement, associated so closely with colonialism could not fail to be infected. There were some to be sure who were so molded by the New Testament's rejection of racism that they saw it for what it was. One of these was J. H. Oldham, the first secretary of the International Missionary Council. In a book written in 1924 called *Christianity and the Race Problem* he threw a sharp challenge to the churches:

> Christianity is not primarily a philosophy but a crusade. . . . Hence when Christians find in the world a state of things that is not in accord with the truth which they have learned from Christ, their concern is not that it should be explained but that it should be ended. In that temper we must approach everything in the relations between races that cannot be reconciled with the Christian ideal.

Yet as we know, racism persists in the church, not to

speak of the world at large. The growing awareness of the destructive effects of this evil, on the oppressed and the oppressing races, has intensified its bitterness and hurt. Who knows how many black and Indian North Americans, and how many Asians and Africans have in understandable resentment rejected not only the white race but also the "white man's God" and have thus shut themselves off from the joy of Christ's presence and the ministry of the church in their lives? The unfaithfulness of the Christian witness at this point is bearing its bitter fruit.

Against this background how can we decry the gestures that our churches have made—and on an international scale the World Council of Churches has made—to demonstrate our Christian support for the battle against racism? The grants that the WCC has made, for medicines, education and welfare, to organizations struggling—violently or nonviolently—for justice for the oppressed races, have shown to the world that the churches, despite their past, are no friends of racism, that they can tolerate violence against injustice when colored as well as white people are in the battle. To millions of people in Africa and Asia the widely publicized WCC grants of 1970, which caused consternation to many Christian people, have restored the credibility of the gospel. In the history of World Council actions, there has probably been none that spoke to the world so eloquently of Christ's concern for the oppressed, of the relevance of Christianity and of the universality of the gospel.

It is a curious fact of the times that the Christian dilemma between rejection of all war and the challenge of injustices to which the only answer seems to be violence appears to be always before us. Non-Christian and Christian thinkers alike pose the question of whether violence can ever solve the problems of society, whether that violence is exercised by rulers or rebels. What shall be the response to injustice of those whose crucified Lord was the supreme example of rejection of a violent response to injustice? How shall we respond to the needs of those others who are caught in the bondage of implacable oppression? This is no new dilemma; but it has never been raised more sharply than today. The pain of choice becomes more bitter when we realize that the leaders of violent and nonviolent liberation movements in our own countries as in other parts of the world have in many cases formed their positions against the background of their Christian understanding of justice and peace and human rights.

A second paradox that characterizes today's world lies in the question of power. Increasingly complex technological and scientific discoveries have expanded the body of knowledge at a geometric rate and made possible exploits that were not dreamed of even a generation ago. The old saying that everyone talks about the weather but no one does anything about it is no longer true. And even inherited human characteristics are not untouchable by the white-smocked geneticists who discuss in hushed tones the possibilities before them to plan and construct the kind of human personality wanted.

But even as this scientific near-omnipotence approaches, we have become less and less confident of our ability to understand the course of human history, much less to determine it. Gone is the confident Victorian poet's dream of building "a new Jerusalem in England's green and pleasant land." Among us is rather the desperate fear that in some moment of inadvertent human failure we may blow our world to nothingness. For if technological power grows, we are by no means sure, in spite of the advertising men, that we can effectively influence the way people live, their value systems, their future. No single event has been more influential in developing this feeling of powerlessness than the war in Vietnam, which, in spite of attempts of both hawks and doves (in their very different ways) to end it, rolled on relentlessly like a classic tragedy. The radical theology of men "come of age" and no longer needing God had its brief career on the stage and is nearly forgotten.

The process of secularization, which has, with man's growing understanding of nature, released him from bondage to its arbitrary powers, is not in its essence antireligious. It is in accord with the biblical record which has rather revealed to man that God is not a projection of the unknown forces of nature; he is the God above nature, who in the Bible is in conversation with man and whose purpose is that man shall be free and responsible for himself and for his neighbor. In a secularized world man can no longer hide from himself; he can no longer "place the blame on nature or on his heritage, or call on God in desperation to fill in the gaps or be a *deus ex machina.* . . . What has emerged is the true character of man as wrapped up in himself individually and collectively (Luther called this *incurvatus in se,* which was his definition of sin)."

Furthermore, as Dr. Potter suggests, secularization has not robbed of its life the human predilection for the creation of idols. The reception by new believers in the West of religions of Asia, and the rise of mystic cults. witchcraft, and astrology show that people are today more animistic than secularized. If another element in modern society is the pointless hedonism and personal struggle for wealth that spells moral decay, still the most important and deceptive idolatry today is the secular religion of the modern political ideology, which gives to some system of social order the absolute values of the transcendent. It is of interest that Marx's mentor, Feuerbach, was entirely aware, as Helmut Gollwitzer points out, of the fact "that when the life for heaven is replaced by a life for earth, then work must replace prayer and politics must replace religion: 'For we must become religious again—politics must become our religion—but that it can only do, if we have a highest target in our sights, which makes politics into religion.' " (*Christian Faith and the Marxist Critique of Religion.* New York: Scribners, 1970. p. 70.) A recent visitor to China, trying to understand theologically the events there, has noted that this new society, which is often thought to be religionless, is in fact thoroughly moralistic and therefore religious in nature. (Neale Hunter in *China: The Peasant Revolution.* R. Wylie, ed. Geneva: WSCF Books, 1972. p. 81 ff.) Others have noted the quasi-religious elements in the structures of all political totalitarianisms.

The predicaments of modern man is that whether he is held in sway by the license of secular individualism with no transcendant values, or by the disciplined fanaticism of the ideological state, the human in him is lost. In the one, society disintegrates; in the other, man is again enslaved. The idolatry of the system is no worse but perhaps no better than the idolatry of the self; in neither is there ultimately any healing for man and his world. Between these two alternatives modern man seems to be helplessly caught. If to Schleiermacher religion was a sense of dependence, to many a modern its heart lies in a sense of lostness. It is "out of the depths" that the cry comes.

Perhaps it is too much to call the third aspect of the context of mission paradoxical, as Dr. Potter does. Paradox or no, however, it is useful to note two contradictory attempts to deal with the inadequacies of culture in process of change. The first is the cultural revolutions in some of the newly independent nations of Asia and Africa, and most prominently in China. These revolutions aim at cultural renewal, sometimes by rejection of the old and at other times by embracing it. But the aim is in all cases the same: to remold the whole of society in an attempt to move men toward the goals of a unified and healthy community. The values and class structures of the past are examined and often repudiated. Pervasive efforts are made to change the ways of thought and living of whole populations.

In Latin America the instrument for the promotion and initiation of radical cultural revolution is *concientization,* the teaching process by which people, particularly the still unsecularized masses, are made aware of their capacity to shape their futures, to change the old social order in order to open the way to progress toward the common goal.

In other continents, particularly in the North Atlantic area, not cultural revolution but counter-culture has appeared. It is, broadly speaking, a rejection by elements, mostly youthful and middle class, of the community of "the individual and collective selfishness of the consumer society, with its cult of quantity over quality, of material affluence over integrity, of mediate experience purveyed by the mass media over the immediate experience of creative and shared self-expression."

The churches have not always recognized the nearness of the many ethically sensitive rebels in the counter-culture to the Christian way, and have failed to understand or accept their criticisms. One reason is simply that the counter-culture has often seen the churches to be corrupt manifestations of cultural-religious conformism rather than revitalizing, renewing forces in society. Another is that the counter-culture in its indiscriminate rejection of all the standards of the establishment has too often flouted the good as well as the merely conventional or the wrong in the establishment's way of life. The rebels too have their blind spots for sin and selfishness.

These are but some of the aspects of today's context for mission. To say that these circumstances isolate the modern from the past generation would be an exaggeration. If that were so, the literature of another age would not be read today. There is that in man which is persistent through every age and in every culture, and it is thus that the Bible speaks to all, from every age and nation. But if we are to speak the word of salvation to today's world, we must interpret the Scriptures so they will be understood by the man who in this age is moved by these currents of history.

3.

What Is Salvation?

What does the word *salvation* mean? The answer is both obvious and obscure. Popularly, what salvation is depends on what one needs. To the prisoner in his cell salvation may simply be an unlocked door. To the fading beauty, a new skin cream. To those who are hungry, a bowl of rice. To the Chinese communist, salvation is the plan for a new society, put into practice. To the soldier in the front lines, the armistice. To the dying, the assurance of heaven.

But none of these definitions approaches in its richness the biblical meaning of the word, so comprehensive that no one and no age can absorb its breadth and depth.

Salvation is forgiveness, redemption, reconciliation, acceptance, peace, joy, security, health, and wholeness. It is a gift an accomplishment, freedom, and servanthood. Building on the theology of the centuries, the report of the study groups that prepared for Bangkok and those in Bangkok expounded the wealth of meaning to be found in the word. One European group, working within the terms of Orthodox theology, found the word *theosis* a particularly rich concept; salvation is the act of God by which he makes man "divine." Another explored the five elements into which the salvation events in the Bible might be broken down: judgment, intervention, victorious rescue, spacious freedom and mission (Michael Green. *The Meaning of Salvation*. London: Hodder and Stoughton, 1965).

Salvation: Personal or Social

Wherever the subject of God's salvation is discussed, however the idea is approached, one problem arises: if salvation is not simply an inner spiritual event, but also has its social life-related aspect, how are these two related? The question can be posed in many ways. How is salvation as change *in* man related to salvation as change *around* him? How is salvation as regeneration, man's "being-born-againness" and therefore his capacity to transcend his environment, related to salvation as transforming or at least maintaining order in the environment? Or, practically, how are evangelism and development, proclamation and social justice related?

Luther had his theology of the "two kingdoms," the kingdom of law and that of grace, of civil rule and gospel ministry. A distortion of Luther has led in some societies to the practical abdication by the church of any constructive social responsibility. Yet Lutheranism in other environments has been deeply concerned with the social order. The medieval compromise has in some societies persisted, with a constant tension between church and state over whose power shall "save" the people. Calvin's attempt to revive a sort of Old Testament theocracy was the converse of the Erastian order in which the head of state was secondarily head of the church, as in England.

Whatever the political and religious structures have

been, an acceptable theological formulation has always been difficult to work out. The tendency to over-emphasize God's saving activity in Christ as a purely spiritual and inner and other-worldly matter has led to the famous description of religion as the "opiate of the people," a comfort to be sure, but hardly an effective force in the struggle for a more just society. The other tendency, to emphasize the social-ethical-political aspect of Christianity to the exclusion of the spiritual, inner element, can make of the church little more than a political party and can lead to the absolutizing, or idolizing of political systems by claiming for them divine authority and support.

The one emphasis spiritualizes and personalizes the message of the Scriptures. It finds in the liberation of the Hebrews from Egypt an allegory of the spiritual life, forgetting that here were real people whom God in history really delivered from slavery to another nation. The other emphasis sees the saving effects of the gospel first of all in social ethics, the improvement of society, the enrichment of life, and finds in the Old Testament prophet rather than the New Testament evangelist the prototype of the Christian preacher.

The relationship between salvation as inner and spiritual and salvation as temporal and social cannot simply be described as casual, the latter the consequence of the former. It cannot be denied that individuals who admit no allegiance to Christ are sometimes by all Christian ethical standards "better" than Christians. And societies with other than Christian beliefs and members have been known to be relatively as "healthy" as Christian societies, as far as we can judge. This phenomenon is explained in three ways.

1. Ethical living, corporate and personal, has nothing to do with salvation; this would make of salvation a completely other-worldly matter.

2. "By their works you shall know them," i.e. anyone who is proximately Christian in his actions is in fact a crypto-Christian: the hidden Christ has come into his life although he may not know it. As with the individual, so with society: even a society that denies religion and aspires only to serve humankind may in fact be a society being saved, within God's orbit. The difficulties with this theology are perhaps too obvious to point out. They include the imposition of the name "Christian" on those who may be quite unwilling to accept it or conversely the relinquishment of any unique claims for the Christian way of salvation. Furthermore it identifies salvation by works rather than by grace—a contradiction in terms.

3. In fact there is a different quality to Christian living, because whatever things may seem externally, the "civil righteousness" (as much a part of human nature as the tendency to sin and based on enlightened self-interest or natural altruism) is qualitatively different from the righteousness of the Christian who lives under the cross and is moved by gratitude for grace received—that is, is responding in love to God's love. The observable goodness of a person or of a social system may have nothing to do with salvation at all—only God knows. Salvation is of God and through the Holy Spirit, who leads to faith in Christ and impels us to lives of love. Although one can cooperate as a Christian citizen with non-Christians in working for improved individual and corporate life, such activity does not in the end have more to do with salvation than taking an aspirin to relieve a headache has to do with health. The difficulty with this position is that it does not seem to take seriously the reality of spiritual and ethical values in society outside the church. This world is after all God's world in which his hand is moving in however hidden a way in all that

is truly productive of peace and love and goodness and justice, all that is healing and saving.

How did the early Christians solve this problem of the relationship of the personal and the social aspects of salvation? They seem to have withdrawn briefly from society to live in their own community until the Lord came. But this experiment in a counter-cultural social salvation did not last long. Countless other attempts at righteous communities have been made; they have been seen as a way of bringing the Kingdom of God among men—of being sure that *here* God's salvation is present. But none have solved the problem. M. M. Thomas's statement (see page 93) is perhaps a step in that direction, but Bangkok cannot be said to have resolved this intractable problem either. It is possible that one reason was the lack of prominence given to the word *love* in our debates. But Bangkok struggled with three other words that seemed to speak of salvation to modern man.

These three concepts of salvation, among many others, have been emphasized in the current discussion. Each of them can be used to describe both the inner, spiritual salvation and the outer, temporal salvation. They are the concepts of *liberation, humanness* and *identity*.

Salvation as Liberation

"Go down, Moses, way down to Egypt's land. Tell Old Pharaoh, 'Let my people go!' " says the Negro spiritual. It sings of the longing of the American Black for liberation. *Liberation* is the poor man's definition of salvation. It is the cry of the powerless, the prayer of the oppressed. What is striking about the spiritual, however, is that its cry for liberation rises from the throats of a liberated people: salvation is here paradoxically demanded by the saved. The slaves in the American South who wrote this song knew their Lord, had accepted his grace, and drew on it day by day in order to live with their oppressors in what were—by accounts of both slave and master—often bonds of tolerance and love. The intensity of the spiritual's cry for liberation bears witness to the fact that the spirit, though freed and saved, still struggles against everything which threatens a fuller experience of that freedom.

Today, when the rights of man are acclaimed as never before but are denied by the political oppression of totalitarian states and racial and economic injustice, it is small wonder that the cry for freedom comes from those enslaved by these social forces, and liberation is seen primarily in a social context. It is among Latin Americans who, like the writers of the spiritual, have a long Christian tradition and have long known the liberation of the spirit, that the most articulate spokesmen for salvation as liberation may be found. Like the slaves, their freed spirits long for a fuller salvation through life in freed societies.

But the cry for liberation is universal. It comes from men everywhere who feel powerless. And it carries the longing for both personal and social liberation.

One black Christian wrote of liberation as the capacity to transcend circumstances, rather than be bound by them:

> In my country I am a second-class citizen, a leper. When I met the man Christ who is God, I became a different person. I had no walls and became a full man. I can give of my culture to others and receive from them. If I was not a Christian I would not be so sensitive to my wholeness as a person. Christianity has opened my eyes to the evil of being made less than a person.

Another black Christian wrote of his need for liberation from the bitterness of resentment:

> In my country, a white shop assistant smiles at her white customers, her face alive and alert. When she turns to me, her face and eyes go blank and she sees not a person but a black. Only by resisting, by fighting back, can I relate to her—and so I quarrel with her. I even hate her. But as a Christian I have to go beyond hate to the love that involves suffering, forgiveness and reconciliation.

Still another black Christian, a man from South Africa, said in Bangkok, "Some see salvation as insurance for a future life. I want a salvation that helps me be whole now." To him wholeness meant release from the constricting laws of apartheid that would make it possible for him and his people to share the benefits of the land equally with white citizens.

But not only the powerless need liberation. It has often been noted that the one who holds another down in the gutter is down in that gutter himself. The hates, the fears, the paralysis that the manipulation of others engenders are also a kind of prison. Salvation is the liberation also from that prison. It comes if we will but see ourselves not as masters but as servants. The price of liberation of white people, the best of the black prophets have proclaimed, is the liberation of the blacks.

Salvation as Humanness

What does it mean to be human? The common response to that question is that it is to be weak: "I'm only human." Or on the other hand omnipotent: "The people," says Mao Tze-tung, "are God." Or to have rights: "I'm a human being!" But biblically to be human is to be created in the image of God—dependent, contingent to be sure, but endowed with a transcendent character derived from God and binding the human person to the Creator. The religious and the atheist alike recognize that man fails to live up to the image he has of himself. That, so to speak, the *fully* human is never attained.

There has been much misuse of the term *humanization* in the discussion of this aspect of the meaning of salvation. One speaks of the "inhuman" working conditions on farm or factory, as if the substitution of mechanical for hand labor or the installation of fluorescent lights and air-conditioning could somehow make the working man more human than he is. One speaks of the "dehumanizing" effects of industrial society and somehow affirms the old heresy of the sinful city and the sanctified rural society. But one group in Bangkok saw that urban industrialization was not the only dehumanizing system. "Private ownership," a report reads, "in urban areas and feudalistic control of land in rural areas deny the poor any possibility of achieving their manhood." The same people who speak of the humanization of society as the provision of better conditions for the poor accuse the wealthy of being underdeveloped humanly speaking. They thus say, paradoxically, that both poverty and wealth are dehumanizing and sound rather like the Marxists who claim that becoming fully human is mainly a matter of the distribution of wealth.

The critics of society who point out the dehumanizing effects of the attitudes which lie behind a society's treatment of individuals or groups are, however, pointing to and undeniable fact: a person often becomes, unless he has a deep inner personhood, that which he is said to be. It is for this reason that anything which denigrates, which restricts or distorts a person's self-image is so deadly. The old epigram that ends "words can never hurt me" is a brave but false saying. For it is the assaults on one's dignity and self-confidence and not the breaking of bones that destroy the human personality and are thus dehumanizing.

But in the most significant sense, the problem of *being* human is precisely that of *becoming* human. Our humanity is attenuated, stunted, perverted by sin—that turning in upon oneself that is rebellion against God, the rupture of human relationships, and ultimately the rejection of one's self. The problem of becoming human is the problem of the renewal of the image of God, through reconciliation with him, the acceptance of forgiveness and the new birth. It is at the same time the problem of reconciliation with one's fellow man, the capacity to live with him as brother, that reconciliation being a mark of the restoration of a relationship with God. "For he who does not love his brother whom he has seen, cannot love God whom he has not seen" (1 John 4:20). In this double reconciliation lies the restoration of one's own sense of personhood.

And all of this begins with what Emilio Castro, the new director of World Mission and Evangelism for the World Council of Churches, called "a personal encounter with Jesus Christ." It is to be lifted by his human example and his divine self-giving; to know that to be human is to know how to love rather than to be loved, to give rather than to have, to suffer rather than to cause suffering, to see in others that creature of God's love that one knows oneself to be, to seek for justice less for oneself than for one's neighbor.

If this be true, to be human, that is to be saved, is to be engaged in the loving, serving struggle against exploitation of people by people, against all forms of oppression—political, economic, social, sexual, racial. It begins with an encounter with Jesus. It continues in the fellowship with him and his human body the church and in self-giving, which is paradoxically the way to fulfillment of one's human potential. For the least, the servant, shall be the greatest.

Salvation as Identity

The air is full these days of psychological terms. One of the most frequently heard and most powerfully emotive is the term *identity*. In this day of mobility, of uncertainty and agnosticism, of loneliness and alienation and all the melancholy consequences of an individualism gone mad, it is the name attached to that which is most basic. To be saved is to find the answer to that elemental question: Who am I?

To this question neither technology nor natural science can provide an answer. The social sciences offer tentative and too often confusing proposals. They do suggest, and rightly, that we find our identities in relation to others. And that it is in lack of human relationships that "lostness" consists. It is the claim of the Christian church to be able to provide the ultimate answer to that question that entitles it to be a sense of universal mission.

The Christian revelation declares that man's primary relationship is to his Creator. We are twice children of God: by creation and by redemption. God has broken through our loneliness in the incarnation. His identification with us in the person of Jesus Christ, the Son of God and man, our brother, has given to us a place beyond as well as in the immanent world. Salvation is to be, to be found, *in Christ*

But our identity is also to be defined in relation to other men, for man is not made to live alone. Salvation is the abandonment of individualism and acceptance of integration in a community. The family of God is a more real family, Jesus said, than the biological one (Matt. 12:46-50). In a different way than that which the institutional theology of early Catholicism intended, the phrase *extra ecclesiam nulla salus* is true—there is no salvation outside the community of faith. One can no more be saved alone than one can be human alone.

A participant at Bangkok said this about his experience in a country where the church is very small:

> In my country, the solidarity of the state religion is tremendous. In becoming a Christian I made myself a second class citizen. I lost my sense of belongingness. I am conscious that I am cut off from my own people like an uprooted tree. The answer of course is for the church to be there to belong to, but in my case the church is not yet strong enough to give the sense of belongingness. The answer is to become more like Christ and accept suffering love and therefore to be liberated from all fetters and give back to the culture all the blessings that come through Christ.

Whatever else this may mean, it certainly means that, as never before in an age of alienation, the Christian community as real community is of the essence of the Christian witness among men. To the extent that the church fails to be a community by which a person can define his or her identity, it fails to be the family of God. It is for this reason that it is, for example, of the greatest importance that in the church women be accepted as full persons, that the barriers of sex, race, social and economic status, and cultural differences that divide community be broken down.

An urgent need to intensify the Christian community's sense of unity, common purpose, and accomplishment has been the major factor in bringing into existence radical Christian communities of all kinds, from that first short-lived communal group in Jerusalem to the Christian communes of the present. To members of such groups the definition of identity that inclusion in the community means may be the most important thing in life, and the source of unlimited courage and power.

Membership in such a community may tempt the Christian to reject the culture around him, to be in other words part of a counter-culture. Some Christians believe that such a counter-cultural position is essential, and they point to the persecuted church of the early days for their justification. A closer reading of the New Testament, however, shows that the early Christians, after that brief experiment, were no counter-culture. Their values and their categories of thought were increasingly influenced by the Greco-Roman world.

For most Christians the temptation is the opposite. The words of Dr. Potter's report apply to most:

> The churches and their missionary activities are caught in the structures of their societies. The failure to cope . . . with the eruptions which have taken place in [recent] years has demonstrated very clearly the captivity of the churches and the missionary agencies to the political, economic, racial and cultural institutions of society. The church which would be the bearer of salvation today needs itself to be saved, liberated from that which is false to the revolutionary, convicting and renewing nature of the gospel.

The relationship of the church to the culture in which it lives is a complex one, as has been suggested above. It is a particularly pressing one these days as new nations of Africa and Asia are recalling with pride their cultural heritage, sometimes giving to it a quasi-religious value. It is important as young churches and old recognize their function as culture-forming and their identity as culture-formed institutions, and it is difficult, not least in countries like North America where cultural and religious pluriformity is not only tolerated but encouraged even as we tend to confuse our loyalties to church and state with each other. A section report in Bangkok includes a useful paragraph:

> It is difficult to describe "the community in Christ in the Holy Spirit" in this context. We played with the concept of the Christian community itself as a counter-culture; but we abandoned this idea because it cut us off too definitely from the communities of men of which we are also a part. Only in extreme cases may we be called to shake the dust of the city from our shoes; usually we shall have to live in a somewhat dialectical relationship, participating with a certain hesitation, identifying ourselves while keeping our critical distance. This dialectic should not hinder us however from being fully engaged with others in the search for justice and freedom. Our identity is in Christ and with him we identify ourselves; by him also we may be withdrawn. The criteria for so tender a relationship are taught us when we let the Scriptures continuously surprise us and keep our communion with the Lord and his people.

What is salvation? Many things, but also at least these three: liberation, humanness, identity.

It is with these understandings of salvation (and the others) then that the church must concern itself; for salvation is the business of the church, its mission in the world.

4.

Elements in Today's Mission: Proclaiming the New Life

What is the aim of Christian mission? In what may be the best short statement to come out of Bangkok, Section III. Church's Renewal in Mission thus defined the aim of Christian mission:

It is our mission

—to call men to God's salvation in Jesus Christ;

—to help them to grow in faith and in their knowledge of Christ in whom God reveals and restores to us our true humanity, our identity as men and women created in His image;

—to invite them to let themselves be constantly recreated in this image, in an eschatological community which is committed to man's struggle for liberation, unity, justice, peace, and fulness of life.

In today's atmosphere there is unquestionably much that is inimical to the pursuit of the evangelistic task. Obdurate and doctrinaire Marxism-Leninism declares again and again that religion as such and Christianity in particular is incompatible with a scientific approach to reality. In the countries where an orthodox Leninist regime is in power, a practicing Christian is to some degree hindered from full exercise of political rights—at least he is excluded from party membership. Public evangelism is forbidden or frowned upon, although freedom of religious belief is guaranteed by constitutional law, and in some Eastern European countries the churches receive substantial aid from public funds as they did before the revolution. It should be added that certain Marxist parties—Castro's in Cuba and some Indian Communists—are ambiguous on the question of religion, and Allende's government in Chile is by no means anti-religious; cultural contexts affect Marxism as they do theology.

But evangelism is a threat not only to Marxist governments. One could name a number of European countries where the dominant church is so closely related to the state that any other form of Christianity labors under restrictions. And there are countries in Asia and Africa where the need for national unity is so strong that any movement to evangelize—because evangelism always tends to divide the citizenry—is seen as a threat to the community and the nation. This phenomenon is not new; it has been an implicit position in the Middle East for centuries.

In the "liberal West" the cultivated atmosphere of the middle classes, which in its individualism places a high value on a pluralistic society, considers it rather poor form to be too insistent on any religious conviction. The ecumenical movement has been correct in its assertion that our diversity and disunity, not to speak of the tendency of churches to prey upon each other, cast doubt upon the evangelist's claim to a unique and life-giving word from God. The rather unpleasant terms *proselytism* and *religious imperialism* have come to be used about evangelism. Even to some devoted Christians, to quote a WSCF paper, "Words like 'evangelism' or 'mission' have now become problematic" (*IRM* Jan. 1970, pp. 28-29).

Nonetheless, as Johannes Hoekendijk has pointed out, there can be no moratorium on evangelism.

> We have, it seems to me, to reject the temptations from both sides. There can be no moratorium: a) in order to arrange things with those who are scandalized by the uniqueness of the Christ event; or b) so that the Christian community will be so 'purified' that it can present itself as a verification of the unverifiable gospel. There seems to me no way out . . . no delay possible . . . no moratorium thinkable. In accepting the gospel one puts oneself in the scandalous position of being an "evangelist of the world in this generation" (*IRM* Jan. 1970, p. 30.

So, in spite of barriers and inhibitions, and sometimes regrettably encouraged by the unchristian motivations of bigotry and the will to power, the churches in the current age are heavily and widely engaged in the evangelistic task.

The watchword to which Hoekendijk refers above is nearly a century old. It challenged the Christian youth of that day to a goal that for the first time in history seemed possible of attainment: "The evangelization of the world in this generation!" Was it indeed realistic? Was it not romanticism? What did it really mean? The great ecumenical and missionary leader John R. Mott in a book published in 1901 defined it negatively:

> Does *not* mean the conversion of the world within the generation *(evangelization* not *conversion).*

> Does *not* imply the hasty or superficial preaching of the gospel.
> Does *not* signify the Christianization of the world.
> Does *not* involve the entertaining or supporting of any special theory of eschatology.
> Is *not* to be regarded as a prophecy.
> Does *not* minimize, but rather emphasizes the importance of the regular forms of missionary work.
> The evangelization of the world in this generation should *not* be regarded as an end in itself. (IRM Jan. 1970, p. 26.)

What then does it mean today? Bangkok suggested one answer:

> Each generation must evangelize its own generation. To work for *church growth and renewal* is the chief abiding and irreplaceable task of Christian mission. (*Report,* Section III. Church's Renewal in Mission)

This statement was presented, like all other section reports, for discussion and reflection by the Conference and referral to the churches, rather than for the kind of adoption that would indicate full approval. A mission executive rose and asked if the phrasing was not too institutional, too church-centered. Was not the focus of evangelism and mission on the world?

Church Growth Evangelism

And indeed (as we have noted in Chapter 2) there is a continuing and significant debate about the place of the church as an institution in God's plan for the world's salvation. Possibly the most interesting and influential school of thinking on evangelism to touch American Protestant overseas work in recent decades has been associated with the name of its tireless proponent,

Donald MacGavran. Church Growth evangelism asserts that the central task and top priority of mission is the numerical growth of the church around the world, for that is the way the largest numbers of people become vitally related to Christ as their savior. It believes that such growth is the prime evidence of vitality and the prerequisite of improvement of society. MacGavran has rightly questioned the traditional highly individualistic approach to conversion. He says that people are best brought into the church not as single converts but in natural sociological groupings—families, clans, tribes. These natural groups, which have often been a barrier to religious change, can be the "bridges of God" if evangelists approach them rightly. A decision for Christ is no less real if it is a decision taken by a group together, in the way that traditional non-Western societies tend to make decisions.

The Church Growth school, in contrast to traditional methodology which tended to undervalue cultures, makes careful use of the science of cultural anthropology. It realistically declares that one should not expect overnight acceptance of the most enlightened New Testament ethics in a new Christian group. Indeed—and here it is criticized—it holds that one of the tools of church growth may be ethnic consciousness, which of course is closely related to—if not the same thing as—racism.

That this is an effective tool for group movements is indisputable, but is it evangelism? Is it possible to encourage conversion on the basis of adherence to a group —that is, to a tribal church—and then declare as the New Testament does that tribalism is contrary to the spirit of Christ in whom there is "neither Jew nor Greek"? Is it a naive assumption that if once the people are in the church, social and ethical change will naturally follow? Has not history proved otherwise?

It was noted at Bangkok that according to testimony from the German Democratic Republic spiritual vitality in the church was growing even as numbers shrank. A section report reads:

> We defined growth as being at the same time the numerical growth of the church and the development of a new man in every person, the rooting of Christians' faith in local realities and their commitment to society. Concerning renewal, we saw that the starting point is in the renewal of man through Christ. We found that certain churches grew numerically whilst others are undergoing both a shrinkage and renewal at the same time. There can be numerical growth without renewal through motivating forces which are foreign to the gospel: such growth is deceptive. On the other hand, every renewal should result in numerical growth, since the power of the gospel is communicative (Section III, p. 7).

The usefulness of Church Growth theology as a critique of the past and as suggestive guidance for work in a declining number of stable societies is accepted. Application of its principles has revitalized many a stalled evangelism program and brought rapid and often healthy church extension, in North America as well as elsewhere. It recognizes the value of community. Yet it builds on the traditional rather than the "new" Christian community. And it is noteworthy that it seems to have little impact in the great cities where the future of much of the world is now being hammered out.

The most radical criticism of Church Growth thinking is made on two other points. The first is that it can pervert evangelism into a numbers game without ethical content. The second criticism, which comes most articulately out of India, has to do with the question of the relation of the institutional church to salvation. "Christian conversion gathers people into the worshipping community, the teaching community, and the community of service to all men," declared the group at Bangkok that studied the meaning of conversion. This was orthodox enough. But the next sentence suggested the possibility of something different from what we traditionally call *church*. "Even if people are not called out of their culture and separated from the society in which they were born, they still will form cells of worship, of reflection, and of service within their original cultures."

M. M. Thomas, in his address at Bangkok, referred more directly to the Indian discussion, which is based in part on the experience of people of Hindu background whose experience of Jesus Christ as Lord is beyond question, but by whom the formal steps to institutional church membership are for any of a number of reasons rejected or neglected.

Dr. Thomas also spoke of the criteria for Christian faith "in a pluralistic age." He spoke of the inadequacy of simple adherence to a religious institution. "God and idols cut across them. The criterion is openness and response to the meaning of life and sense of the transcendent as revealed in the person of Jesus Christ." The criterion is not "the choice between religion and atheism. Religion may be idolatrous, and atheism no more than a denial of idols and the affirmation of an undefined transcendence like the unknown God of the Athenians, is open to the reality of the transcendent humanity of the cross, like the atheism of Nehru or some Marxist humanists." He notes that Professor Hans Küng has recently suggested that the criterion of faith could be that the believer in some form acknowledge the person of Jesus as "decisive for life," that is, decisive for the "realization of the ultimate meaning of life and its fulfillment here and hereafter." He continues the questioning in a way that should be most threatening to the confessional bodies in the Christian family that are most committed to the sacraments and the catholicity of the church as an institution, and where he himself is at home. But strangely enough these views have been attacked most sharply by theologians who usually tend to emphasize the decisive importance of the personal encounter and the unimportance of institutions. (For a slightly abridged version of Dr. Thomas' address, see *Study Helps,* Section D.)

The Scope of World Mission

Commenting on the question of God's saving activity outside the church, Section I in Bangkok began with the fact of God's activity in all creation. His activity is in some sense redeeming as well as providential; for these two aspects of his action in a fallen creation, though they may be distinguished, cannot be separated. This fact, however, gives us no right to build a theology about God's hidden work. "Our preoccupation is with the revealed Christ."

> The manifestations of God are always surprising. Basically there is no realm of life and no situation where he cannot reveal himself. We believe that he is present in his whole creation. But we do not want to make this belief an operative principle for pointing out where he is at work, lest we say: here is the Messiah, or there is the Messiah, when he is not there.

> Although we expect his presence with men and although we know that the Spirit translates the groaning of all mankind into prayers acceptable to God, we believe that this insight is more a reason

to worship his freedom than an invitation to build theological theories. Our preoccupation is with the revealed Christ and with the proclamation of him as he has been made known to us. Scripture tells us that Christ identifies himself with the poor and that the Spirit translates the groaning of men; this may indicate the direction in which we are invited to move but it does not give us power to pinpoint the details of his presence. The observation that Christ-like action and insights which we know from the Gospels are also present among other groups does not give us the right to claim such groups for Christ; it should lead us deeper into the process of conversion and bring us to worship our Lord even more humbly. He asked us to follow him, not to spy on him.

Where is the mission field today? "Faith no longer comes from the West," read a headline on a story about Bangkok. The slogan "Mission on Six Continents" was headlined at another world mission conference in Mexico City in 1963. The idea of a white Christian West bringing the gospel to the pagan peoples of the less developed world dies hard. Our North American churches, where they use the words *world mission,* rarely include their own country in the *world.* The International Missionary Council dealt with church organizations in Asia and Africa, but with agencies for overseas work in Europe and North America. The department of a world association of churches which worked with the churches of Asia and Africa was called the Department of World Mission until 1970, and when reorganization came, the word *mission* was omitted from a new department that also included concern for Europe and the Americas, in part because some churches there did not like to be identified with "mission."

On this matter the Bangkok meeting was clear. Ecumenical conferences seldom make policy—they report it. So when Dr. Emilio Castro hailed the "end of a missionary era and the beginning of world mission" he reflected a pervasive feeling. The point was not that the work of evangelism in Asia, Africa, and Latin America is done. Whatever may be said about the penetration of the gospel in some identifiable form in almost every country, the fact remains that there are still vast needs. The great populations of Asia are largely unreached. The gospel can come to the Chinese people now only through a tiny, struggling and disorganized Christian community, for foreigners neither are nor can expect to be admitted to live and work as representatives of the Christian church in the People's Republic in the foreseeable future. The need to strengthen the Christian witness in the traditional continents of "mission" remains urgent because so many have not yet heard.

It is also pressing because of those who have. And in spite of the weakness of the Christian moral as well as verbal witness, the gospel is attracting throngs to follow Christ. In the Buddhist stronghold of Thailand, the Protestant Church of Christ is in the midst of an awakening after years of no growth and is in the midst of a campaign to double its membership in four years. The churches in neighboring Indonesia and in parts of India continue to grow rapidly. In South Korea half of the men in the army are now reported to be baptized, the result of energetic work done largely by chaplains. Christians may number less than 10% of the population, but in that eclectic country they form the dominant religious group. Yet the church in the vast continent of Asia will long, probably indefinitely, be a small minority. The prayers of the world church must be for its faithfulness.

In Africa the situation is different. David Barrett, a

student of church life and growth there, predicts that 350,000,000 Africans or half of the population will be Christian by the year 2000. This will make Africa the world center of Christianity, for the North Atlantic countries, which in any event will be smaller in population than Africa by the year 2000, are also losing rather than gaining in effective numbers of Christians. Barrett notes that keeping up with African church growth will require a tremendous investment of both money and people to provide the institutions, the leaders, the parish pastors, and lay workers. The demand, he says, will be on an unprecedented scale (*IRM* Jan. 1970, p. 39f.).

An Ethiopian Lutheran church has recently done some shorter term planning. In the last several years its growth has averaged over 15%; in 1970 it was 26%. The leadership has calculated that between 1971 and 1975 it will need 137 more pastors and 1000 unordained workers. Its schools and training programs are inadequate, and it calls for help.

But some church people are asking if the help that is being given to some of the older and more stable churches in Africa is not detrimental rather than helpful. It has not escaped their notice that among the most rapidly growing churches and those that seem to be more closely related to the African soil are churches which receive no outside help at all. They include some churches of the Pentecostal type, others that are curious blends of African religion with Christianity.

But the prime example is the Church of Jesus Christ on Earth Through the Prophet Simon Kimbangu, which in 1970 became a member of the World Council of Churches. The Kimbanguist Church came into being because a young Christian against his will obeyed a vision to preach and to heal in Jesus' name. For a brief six months beginning in April 1921 he was the center of a remarkable awakening movement. Then the colonial government, which could not tolerate any such popular movement, threw Simon Kimbangu into prison, where he died thirty years later. But led by his wife and later his sons, at first secretly, the church grew without missionary aid or foreign funds. It has had to find its own way of organization, finance, worship life, and biblical interpretation. Conservative in faith and discipline, antiracist and nonviolent, it now works in a dozen countries and is said to have a constituency of four million people.

In the light of such evidence it is perhaps not surprising that at Bangkok and elsewhere the proposal has been made that a "moratorium" on missionaries and foreign funds might give some churches a chance to find their identity in their own cultures. It has happened before, in wartime emergencies, but is it feasible in normal times? So far there has been no rush to try. The more usual practice has been to withdraw missionaries and financial support gradually.

Missionaries East and West

The missionary movement lives then in a paradoxical situation. On the one hand the unfinished task calls for more money and people than are available to the churches of Africa and Asia, and there is an honest call for both support and "laborers for the harvest." On the other hand there is the equally honest conviction that large doses of foreign funds and leadership are by no means the only answer, or even the answer at all, to the needs of a dynamic missionary church; for if outside aid ties the church to the church universal and may ease its way, it also may prevent the young church from firm rooting in its local soil.

The problem epitomized here is one of the most perplexing and persistent in the whole history of missions. It is aggravated when great economic and cultural differences between foreign missionaries and their national colleagues exist—and they usually do.

Yet there was not at Bangkok nor is there elsewhere any undervaluation of the foreign Christian, whether a professional missionary or not. They are a link with the church universal, and they bring with their fresh influence from outside both encouragement and criticism. The concern at Bangkok was that so far the traffic has been so heavily one way. One looks therefore with hope on the growing number of missionaries who are sent by the churches of the Third World. A recent study, to the surprise of most, calculated that there are now some 3000 church workers who have been sent to work outside their own countries or at least across cultural-linguistic lines. Their numbers are growing. And we may see more of them on our continent. For if the emphasis on "world" mission on six continents does not indicate the completion of the task of the evangelization of Asia and Africa, it is a clear call for help from the churches of old "Christendom."

It may not be a surprise, and yet it always comes as a shock to hear a pastor from eastern Europe say, "Jesus is becoming an unknown name for most of the younger people in our country." At Bangkok a delegate from the German Democratic Republic rose in exasperation to plead with the Conference. "Why is it that when we from the socialist countries come to ecumenical meetings, we are here as if we were not here. You do not take Marxism seriously!" This somewhat inchoate eruption was not a plea for a Christian crusade against communism. That was as far from the speaker's mind as revolt against Rome was from St. Paul's. What she wanted was that the challenge of Marxism to Christianity not be ignored, that we think together about how to witness to Christ in a socialist and secular society, that we learn to understand the forces at work—in a word, that we think of salvation in that context which today includes so large a part of the world's peoples.

The problem of Western societies, including those of North America, is not this one, but the dominance of a secular liberal culture whose values invade the church. Why is it that our youth find the churches sterile and seek salvation in esoteric cults? Why is the Jesus Movement to so large a degree outside the churches? Has Jesus become unreal within them? Could the vitality of an African or Asian witness, tested in a minority situation, sure that the answers to life are not found in laboratories, and sure of the immanent presence of the Spirit among men, be able to convert us again from our theological bickering and half-committed lives? At Bangkok it was clear that many of them thought so.

It was clear, too, that they thought that North Americans needed a prophetic word from them about our worship of wealth, our racism, our power, our pride, and above all about our lack of commitment to the world. And they believed that they were needed because North American Christians were not speaking that prophetic word. They see most of us in the church as unwilling to break our alliance with a complacent society, to call on our fellow-citizens to pay the price of economic and social justice at home and in international affairs. They see our competitiveness sometimes marring even our own family life; and our concern for others in the world all but stopping at our borders. They see that through the power we wield by our wealth, our propaganda, our political authority, we impose our ways on a fascinated but fearful world. And that our churches for the most part are indifferent. About things like this our fellow-Christians from overseas want to speak to us. What does conversion to Christ mean if it does not mean conversion to the cause of the poor and needy?

We in North America have missionaries, religious and secular, throughout the world. We have shared much that is good with the world, and with the good we have also exported our society's problems. We have been accused of being unable to receive. It is time now that we listen and think and thank God for the prayers and the ministry of our fellow-Christians to us.

Still we should need no word from overseas to tell us that our cities and our countryside need the gospel of Christ. Every newspaper brings us fresh word to the bondage in which our people are held, of the false deities to which we bow down, and of their destructive results on individuals and on society. Alcoholism and drugs, crime on the streets and in government, conscienceless exploitation of man and of nature, poverty in the midst of plenty—all these are evidence of our perversion and our helplessness. From these the gospel can bring us release and cleansing.

The Nature of Religious Dialog

A discussion of evangelism must not close without a comment on method, and especially some comments on dialog. At the close of the colonial era, when the church's institutional authority began to wane, we began to look more closely at ourselves and our way of meeting those of other faiths. We have discovered that all too often our witness to him has not reflected the fact that at the heart of Christ's ministry was not the goad but the cross, not domination but self-giving. We have not always come to those of other faiths in a spirit of receiving as well as giving, in humility recognizing that they too search for God's salvation. We have not seen the altars "to an unknown God." We have seldom remembered D. T. Niles' definition of an evangelist as one beggar telling another where to find bread. We have not always "reasoned with" those we encounter, as St. Paul and all the greatest missionaries have done. From this self-examination has arisen the concern for dialog.

But what is religious dialog? Some Christians fear that dialog with men of other faiths is a *betrayal* of mission. Conversely, there are those of other faiths who suspect that it is simply a *new tool for mission*. It is, in the true sense, the attempt at mutual understanding and mutual sharing of faith and need. "Until a man has been tempted by the insights of another man's faith, he has not truly understood it," said Walter Freytag. Nor can he truly minister to that man. And until one has openly and honestly shared with another not only the formal theology but also the deepest personal testimonies and problems of one's own faith, he has not honestly witnessed to it.

The late Danish missionary theologian Erik W. Nielsen sometimes privately told of a personal experience he was too sensitive to tell publicly. It may express better than a definition does what dialog is. He was visiting India in the hot season, and after an exhausting schedule he found time to accept the invitation of a Brahmin friend to spend a week in his summer home in the hills. The two men agreed that they would spend the week in meditation, prayer, and conversation, each participating as he could in the religious life of the other. So they were together in reading, in prayer, in talk, and in silence. As the week wore on, Erik Nielsen was increasingly uncomfortable. He was moved by the deep devotion, the authenticity, the serenity, and wisdom of his Hindu friend, and in contrast felt keenly his own doubts, his inarticulate and groping testimony to the meaning of Jesus to him, and what he felt to be his moral and spiritual shallowness. He left his Brahmin friend at the end of the week shaken and questioning, not his own faith in Christ but the propriety of claiming any sort of uniqueness for the Christian faith in the presence of a man in whom the Spirit of God seemed so obviously to be at work. Many months later, after a long silence, he got a letter from his friend. "Today has been a very special day for me," it read. "During the week we were together last summer I saw in you something I had looked for all my life. Today, you will be glad to hear, I was baptized."

5.

Elements in Today's Mission: Improving the Common Life

Outside the church and inside it good solid citizens are asking a simple critical question: why doesn't the church stay where it belongs? What they really mean is, shouldn't the church stay out of political and economic questions? Is it not these days becoming so preoccupied with problems of racism and poverty and social structures and political injustice and a thousand other things that theologians don't understand that its real business is forgotten? Should the church not leave politics and economics to the citizens and the businessman and stick to heaven and hell and the Ten Commandments?

The concern is not entirely unjustified. All too often, on the one hand, the church's involvement in this world's affairs has been ineffectual because it has been limited to two things: the pastor's attempt to be "relevant" on Sunday mornings, and pronouncements on social issues from headquarters. The church, that is the people, understand that their faith affects private morality, but only the laws of the state set the standards and direction for public conduct. (Charity is another matter—we are only beginning to realize how political charity is.)

And on the other hand, as Professor Paul Minear has reminded us, "It is all too easy for our thoughts about salvation to become earth-bound. We assume that political and economic needs are the most basic, and that the frustration of these needs is most intolerable. The more desperate becomes the struggle against war, slavery and injustice, the more restricted the horizons of the soldiers. . . . So obsessed men become with daily crises that they lose touch with perennial realities." (Paul Minear, "Biblical Essays on Salvation," mimeographed, *WCC/CWME* 72/92) The hope of heaven that the church alone teaches is man's best defense against cynicism and despair.

The Church as a Political and Economic Force

But having said this, the question is still the wrong one. The church never has been where it is supposed to stay—out of the realm of politics and economics. Jesus was a political figure, one who rejected leadership of a revolution but died by order of a Roman governor because he was accused of being dangerous to the civil order. One of the first acts of the church was to establish a commune. And if that did not last long, what did last was a sense of mutual concern and economic support for the needy that has marked Christians ever since.

The church has always had political influence. At first it was persecuted because it was a subtle threat to the foundations of the Empire. Then for centuries and until very recent times it has provided religious sanction for civil order—from the Holy Roman Empire to the European kingdoms to the American republics. The church has supported our nationalisms and affirmed our political mythologies. It has worked for peace and justice, and it has blessed our wars. It has given more than tacit approval to an economic system whose insatiable competitive demand is seen now to threaten to bring the whole ecological system down around our ears, to use up the world, as it were.

But when from time to time the church is critical of the established order, her people become uneasy and the questions again arise: Should the church get into politics? Should the church get into economics?

The quiescence of the church in the face of economic injustice brought forth a Karl Marx, who arose because religion of his day was indeed politically and economically effective, but effective as an opiate, to help people tolerate injustice, rather than to cure it. The quiescence of the churches in this century permitted the rise of a Hitler, and the answer to the question, "How could Hitler rise in a Christian country?" is that the churches agreed with him when he said that they had no business in politics and economics. Some who disagreed, including a Bonhoeffer, died interfering as the church in politics, and today they are revered as heroes.

The church cannot get out of politics and economics, because God is interested in such things as freedom, justice, peace, health, and community among people. Politics and economics have to do with precisely these things. The question is not whether the church belongs there. It is *how it functions* there. Let us briefly note what Jesus did as one concerned about the whole man, and then ask what that implies for our age.

The biblical understanding of salvation is commonly expressed in words and figures that speak of restoration. One is redeemed, healed, set free, given sight; one's hunger is satisfied and thirst is quenched; one's wounds are bound up and one's tears are wiped away. Our Lord, as he met the needs of the multitudes and the individuals who came for help, restored them to life and health. But despite his concern for the crowd's well-being and although he sharply criticized the injustice of his own people's leaders, he refused to lead a movement to establish a new social order. He preached the coming of another kingdom, which, he declared, was a kingdom not of this world. He had no intention of establishing his power by violence or the threat of it. His was a kingdom to be established by love, self-giving, by offering salvation, not control. And the cross became its symbol.

But at another level, the level of the here and now, Jesus gave an example of direct response to immediate needs of people. He fed the hungry and he healed the sick. He commanded His disciples to do the same. If Jesus made it clear that his kingdom was not of this world, he also made it clear that the kingdom was there where the sick were healed and the blind received their sight and where the good news was preached (Luke 7:18-23).

What does this concern of the Master for all the needs of man mean? How does the church act as his body today?

You are a Christian pastor and you visit a remote village in Africa. As the children crowd around, you see evident signs of malnutrition. Looking around the countryside you are not surprised, for the fields seem badly tilled and unproductive, and there are signs of drought as well. You distribute vitamin pills and you empty your pockets for the purchase of food. And you preach and teach.

But you are not satisfied because you know that this will not solve the problem. On your next visit you bring an agricultural adviser along because the obvious need is more food production. You also think of the future and of a school, for illiteracy means convervatism; it is a major barrier to change. Only literacy can open the future to these children. If you are at all sophisticated, you know that your earlier gift of food has begun a process, and what you are now contemplating will further that process of social and cultural change whose end you cannot envision. The agriculturist takes a cursory look at soil, water resources, and crops. He notes, among other things, that there are no fruit trees, that the soil is exhausted, and that some terracing would lessen water runoff. He makes some recommendations on these matters to the village elders, and you begin to talk of a school.

On the third visit you have some plans for a school, and the agriculturist has some drafts for an irrigation system which will bring a greater quantity of water to some of the valley land. He notes that nothing has been done in tree-planting, fertilizing, or terracing. The villagers are evasive when asked why. But it eventually comes out that the land tenure system provides that every three years the land, which is communally owned, is reapportioned, so that in a lifetime each villager may have a chance to till the choice fields in the valley. Anyone who improves his land is likely to have it taken away the next year. Consequently no one plans for the long term. The problem is not technological; it is political. And suddenly the church's mission has to do with politics.

In another country the problem is that almost all of the land is owned by great landowners, whose wealth is based on a half share of all crops, and who have no pressing need to increase the crop yield, although the illiterate tenants live at bare subsistence level. Land reform here is the only answer—again a political matter.

In both instances the mission of the church cannot be less than to bring political and economic change. In Both instances that implies cultural change as well. It implies the opening of people's minds, and it implies conflict. It may (and this is the really difficult question) imply violent conflict—for not every country is governed by the will of the majority and not every landlord gives up his holdings voluntarily. And—to bring this simple illustration to the international level—not every wealthy nation will willingly yield its political and economic control over others. Canadians are keenly aware of economic domination from the south. All North Americans should understand why people from still farther south tend to look on us as exploitative landlords and profiteering factory owners.

If democratic processes and negotiated change, if the preaching and teaching ministry of the church, are fruitless, can the Christian mission support violent revolution? The Colombian priest Camilo Torres thought so. He declared that he was a revolutionary, not in spite of, but because he was a priest. And he died under the guns of the police.

Most of us would disagree with Torres, some because we are pacifists, but more of us because we believe violence rarely justifies the cost. Violence is the companion of hate and fear, not of love—and of power, not justice. But if we deplore violence, are we pledging our lives in some equally costly way to seek help for the needy and justice for the oppressed? How may we do so? There are several ways, all of them more or less political.

The first is the obvious one of direct contribution of money and effort to meet the needs of people who struggle just to survive. The Christian has always seen care for the poor, the helpless, and the chronically ill as his responsibility. Sister Teresa's care for the homeless dying in Calcutta has rightly been acclaimed as the very epitome of Christian love and rightly praised by all who have a sense of what real goodness is. If she has had any political affect, it has been that of calling the attention of the world to its poor—and that is an effect not to be undervalued.

Second, the churches have long been engaged in what is now called development—the introduction of new means of livelihood and social organization. Missionaries introduced the cocoa industry to Ghana; they taught cottage industries in India, carpentry in Indonesia and coffee planting in New Guinea. Institutional education was once the churches' most important activity outside the parish. Today, although governments have increasingly assumed the burden of formal education, the churches are called upon for the kind of teaching and advice that helps people meet social change.

The mushrooming of cities calls for our unprecedented efforts. "On the pampas," said a priest in Buenos Aires to a visitor in a conversation about Catholic-Protestant cooperation, "a single padre could easily care for a parish of 5000 souls, for life went on in its unchanging pattern and the people's simple faith was undisturbed. But when they come to the city (which they do at the rate of a thousand a day) their meager understanding is not enough, and their shallow roots in Christianity no longer hold." He was speaking of a problem that is common.

A conception of salvation that gives hope for the afterlife and comfort in the difficulties of this age seems acceptable, and indeed is a "saving" faith where poverty and illness and exploitation are the normal order of things and are not even sensed as oppressive, where there is often no sense of indignation or bitterness: this is the lot that God has given. But when visions of new possibilities in life dawn, and the new burdens of a strange, unaccustomed pattern of life bear down relentlessly on his shoulders, the new migrant to the city is no longer satisfied by or even interested in a gospel that points to a vague future. Hope lies elsewhere; salvation if it is to be salvation must ease today's burden. The church's saving action is in the crowded streets and humble tenements of the new city dweller, in the industrial personnel offices, at the organizer's desk, and the counselor's table. The Christian congregation, as the Pentecostal churches have taught us repeatedly, can be a refuge and a home for the new city dweller.

But it is more than that. It is a political force for the whole community. The problems of Christian service in an urban society illustrate most effectively the way in which simple concern for food and clothing and shelter and health care and security lead the church inescapably into the third kind of service to people: direct political activity. It is the political system that provides or blocks the provision of these things to the people of the city. It is the political system which can assure justice or oppression, opportunity or disaster for the poor. If we recognize this fact in our cities, then it is also credible that at a national or an international level as well, men's hopes for freedom and community and future are affected by the church in large degree as the church can affect the political structures. If the church would serve, it must deal in politics. And if in politics, then in economics.

Consider, for example, the case of Namibia, better known by the name used by its colonial ruler as Southwest Africa. Namibia is today occupied by the Republic of South Africa in defiance of both the United Nations and the World Court. South Africa, while it controls the country, is extracting its mineral resources and allowing foreign corporations to do so, using the labor of the Namibian people trapped by South Africa's apartheid laws.

The most important metal mining company is the Tsumeb Corporation, which is controlled by two American corporations, American Metal Climax and the Newmont Mining Corporation. (The data which follow, and further details, are presented and documented in a booklet called "Namibia: United States Corporate Involvement" by Winnifred Courtney and Jennifer Davis, published by The Africa Fund, 164 Madison Ave., New York, and the World Council of Churches, 1972.)

The Tsumeb mine has now produced about $1 billion worth of metals. The return on investment is a closely guarded secret, but some impression of the profitability of the operation can be obtained from the following available data. The purchase price of the mine, already fifty years old in 1964, was under $3 million. In 1970 the corporation produced $71 million worth of metals, made a profit of $26 million, paid taxes of $14 million to the South African government, which used at least a part of these taxes to maintain and extend its police control over the country. The 1200 white workers in the company were paid at a rate that provides for one of the two or three highest standards of living in the world. The five thousand African workers averaged $29.64 per month, plus food, shelter and equipment. All but a handful of them are recruited on contracts, must stay in compounds without their families for a year before returning to their homes, where their families must stay. Their level of income is about one-twentieth of that of white miners. The African labor earned about $1.8 million excluding food, shelter and equipment for the year 1970. How much of this went back to the company stores in payment for the things that single men in barracks buy to fill their spare time is not known. In any event, these wages are the only part of the operation that Namibians share, since profits, taxes, and operating expenses go to the credit of American capital and industries, white management, and South African interests.

It would appear from available data that within the next decade or two the Tsumeb mine will be exhausted. The patrimony of the Namibians will have shrunk by perhaps $2 billion worth of metals, which will have enriched the industrial nations, primarily the United States. The Namibian people will have received in personal income (if the 1970 figures are typical) about 3% of the value of these metals, plus the value of whatever monies have been spent for the real welfare of the country and not on maintaining an illegitimate foreign regime.

It is difficult to distinguish an economic operation of this kind, supported as it is by the armed force of a tyrannical government, from armed robbery. This is an extreme case of profitability and racial injustice and resource exploitation. Yet it typifies the attitude of the industrial powers toward the developing world, less malevolent than uncomprehendingly indifferent to that world's good. Is it to be wondered at that there are expropriations from time to time? Is it right for governments to protect interests of this kind? Can the church do anything less than protest? To the wealthy and powerful nations of the earth the ministry of the church cannot but be a ministry of judgment. It is its task to speak to those in the management of public affairs about injustices.

How is this done? Sometimes by the power of demonstrative action. In August 1971 the World Council of Churches announced its withdrawal of investments from banks and from corporations doing business in South Africa. The action had long been debated, and there were many who thought this action showed a rather exaggerated and self-righteous attitude. Yet how could the Council protest racist exploitation in South Africa if it shared in the profits of that exploitation? Would it not be like the deacon who bewailed the immorality of the day but leased out his property to the operator of the local bordello?

A Catholic missionary society provided another example of demonstrative action recently. In a costly witness to Christian integrity and a protest against injustice, the White Fathers in May 1971 withdrew all their missionaries from Mozambique. After 25 years of work in the colony they found that the ambiguity of trying to serve Africans and support a Portugese colonial regime was no longer to be tolerated. Four hundred years earlier the church had made its first agreements with Portugal for church-state cooperation in missions. Now one society declared that this arrangement belied the gospel. We may expect that the echoes of that declaration will not easily fall silent.

Sometimes, a Bangkok section believed, political change requires the exercise by the church of political power. "Speaking of salvation realistically, we cannot avoid the question of the proper means. We will produce no economic justice without participation in, and use of, economic power. We will win no political freedom without participation and discriminating use of political power" (Sec. II).

The Witness of a Servant

Yet it was not agreed that the church is to become a power bloc. A Greek bishop warned the assembly eloquently of the delusions of power. Historically, he pointed out, the quest for power has always justified itself on the basis of a quest for justice, and inevitably the attainment of power has ended in corruption. Realistically, the church has never known how to use political power, and is not in any event today in the position to wield power. But above all theologically the church denies its nature if it seeks power. For the nature of the gospel is that it gives, it serves, it empties itself. Christians have lived at their best, he said, in times of powerlessness. It is by its *martyria,* its witness both to judgment and grace, that the church works, not by the manipulation of power. But if it fails to witness, then it is like salt without savor.

The church's ability to affect public affairs depends less on pronouncements from headquarters than on the Christian understanding of its people and the people's willingness to use their political and economic power as citizens. A Washington senator once asked a New York church official who had come to plead for certain legislation on whose behalf he spoke. "I know you don't speak for your membership," he said, "because they are my constituents and nine out of ten would disagree with you." Unless we know what is right and are committed to it, we cannot act effectively to do the right.

One wonders therefore if in the last analysis there is any work of higher priority, not only for the ultimate salvation but for man's salvation in the here and now, than that activity which is the unique function of the church, the placing before the world of the offer of life in Jesus Christ and his claim to our obedience. For response to his goodness provides motivation, and by our thoughtful obedience to him our values are converted. It is in conversion to the life of discipleship to him that we learn to live with others, to love them as ourselves and to become as servants. It is in the learning of the meaning of Jesus' servanthood that we discover what it is to be servants in this day. And it is as servants that Christians, and the church, live out their mission of salvation. The church has been given a unique instrument for personal and social change—the gospel.

The church in politics? Whatever our disagreements on methods, one can only hope so. For politics is how society directs and controls the life of the community. If politics is left to those for whom politics is everything, it is as inevitable as the coming of night that politics will become totalitarianism of the right or of the left. The church's witness to the laws of a just and merciful God of all men is the best assurance we can have of a society where there is freedom and love and justice, that is to say, a society where God's saving grace can work.

6.

An Affirmation of Salvation

What remains to be said? A great deal, but most of all the declaration that salvation is a matter to be celebrated, to be laughed and shouted and sung about. For it is what God has done for us and in us for now and eternity.

For some the best memory of Bangkok will be the hours given to group Bible study. These sessions helped them to experience anew the community of faith and the power of the gospel. One group worked out an Affirmation of Salvation Today, and the whole assembly shared in the joy of that common statement. It summarizes as well as anything can what this book has tried to say:

As we have met together in this fellowship,
we have experienced the joy of the living Christ,
and have been renewed and challenged
by the mutual faith one of another.

We have been deeply conscious of our failures
in obedience to our Lord

and our blindness to the ways he sets before us.
We are moved by a profound feeling of penitence
which both pains us
and frees us for Christ's renewal.

Over and above our distress
at the problems and perplexities of the world,
and our confusion about the structures and role of
   the church
we see the shining of the Light
which no darkness can quench.

With gratitude and joy we affirm again
our confidence in the sufficiency of our crucified and
   risen Lord.
We know him as the one who is, who was and who
   is to come,
the sovereign Lord of all.

To the individual he comes with power
to liberate him from every evil and sin,
from every power in heaven and earth,
and from every threat of life or death.

To the world he comes as the Lord of the universe,
with deep compassion for the poor and the hungry,
to liberate the powerless and the oppressed.
To the powerful and the oppressors he comes
in judgment and mercy.

We see God at work today
both within the church and beyond the church
towards the achievement of his purpose
that justice might shine on every nation.

He calls his church to be part of his saving activity

both in calling men to decisive personal response to his Lordship
and in unequivocal commitment to the movements and works
by which all men may know justice
and have opportunity to be fully human.

In joyous trust in Christ's power and victory
we can live with freedom and hope
whatever the present may be.

The Lord is at hand.

Study Helps

A. Twenty Questions

It has been said that one fool can ask more questions than fifty wise men can answer. Here are a few for starters.

1. St. Paul was a very stubborn missionary, but he could also be very flexible. Where should the church today be flexible, where stubborn?

2. If the point of our Christianity is not the salvation of our souls from punishment, what is it? Is salvation the objective or the consequence of commitment to Christ?

3. It has been noted that, during a century of Christian missions in China, missions brought many new things to Chinese life: Western education, medicine, etc. But society as a whole disintegrated. Then came the People's Republic and within a few years tremendous advances were made in education, health, and economic development and most of all in the resurgence of national unity and confidence. Some have suggested that not the church but Maoism is God's instrument for China's salvation. If this is true, what are the implications? If this is not true, where does the misunderstanding lie?

4. The Christian church is repeatedly accused of being *bourgeois*. Is this true of your parish? It is also sometimes called the "tool" of the ruling classes. Have you ever known this to be true?

5. Much of the church's international work with refugees is undertaken with the cooperation, financial and otherwise, of secular, government agencies. The price of such cooperation is that this kind of work must be divorced from evangelism, i.e., it must be secular in form. Should the church regard this as a problem or not?

6. If you had been a contemporary of Karl Marx, would you have agreed that religion was an "opiate for the people"? Would you make the same judgment today?

7. Mussolini is remembered today as (among other things) the one who made the trains run on time. Is this fact a relevant piece of evidence of the "goodness" of Fascist Italy?

8. What is the nature of Christ's presence in the whole cosmos? Can one conclude that if Jesus Christ is everywhere then everything that is, is good? Why not?

9. In a certain hospital one of the doctors is in a wheelchair, permanently crippled. But she has been said to be the most healthy personality in the place. What does this say about health? About salvation?

10. "Sticks and stones may break my bones, but words can never hurt me." True or false?

11. Who are you? Does it matter if you know or not? How do you define yourself? What does that say about you?

12. How many words and phrases can you list that express the meaning of salvation to you?

13. How would you propose to resolve the contradiction in the statement, "I believe in church unity, but I also think we should all worship and believe within our own different cultures"?

14. Does the Bible anywhere promise that some day Christianity will replace all other faiths? In some countries almost all the people are members of one church. Does this seem to affect the life of the nation for good or ill?

15. What may be some valid reasons for some young people's lack of interest in the church in your community? Does this disinterest mean lack of interest in Christ?

16. Billy Graham recently wrote: "God has called me to be a New Testament evangelist, not an Old Testament prophet." How valid is that distinction for a preacher?

17. There are those who say, "If the church will just worry about changing men's hearts, the improvement of society will take care of itself." What is right and what is wrong about this statement?

18. It was recently noted that the problems of salvation are all to be found concentrated in the experience of the North American Indian people. Can you apply this statement in your own community?

19. Does the fact that Jesus refused to lead an insurrection have any significance for the Christian's attitude toward revolution? Toward violence?

20. If you had $100,000 to spend in some Christian action in India, how would you use it? Would you use it for the same purpose in the south side of Chicago? Why or why not?

B. Bible Study Suggestions

In early 1972 a group of biblical scholars of various traditions met to consider the biblical understanding of salvation. From that consultation arose the following selection of Bible passages, chosen to present different perspectives on the theme. The list is of course not definitive; but it has proved a rich quarry for those who in Bangkok studied and meditated on them.

From servitude to service: Exod. 1:8-21; 3:7-12; 19:3-6; 20:1-3

From despair to shouts of joy: Ps. 30:1-12

Salvation by the power of God: Ps. 79:1-13

Two agents of salvation: Isa. 42:1-9; 45:1-8

Salvation in the face of judgment: Amos 5:4-25

Forgiveness and health: Matt. 9:2-8

The Messiah and his kingdom: Matt. 4:13-25. Luke 4:17-30

Salvation in the name of Jesus: Acts 4:1-22

Salvation as gift and as hope: Rom. 3:21-26; 8:18-39

The plan and the price of salvation: Eph. 2:1-22

Salvation in and for love: 1 John 4:7-21; 5:1-4

Salvation and self-satisfaction: Rev. 3:14-22

The celebration of salvation: Rev. 18:21-24; 19:1-10

C. For Further Reading

The reader or teacher looking for more fresh material is advised to consult the Friendship Press catalog on *Why Mission Today?* —materials for 1973-74. Materials include books, audio-visuals and other teaching materials for adults and youth. Friendship Press materials are distributed by most denominational publishers, or write:

Friendship Press Distribution Office
P.O. Box 37844
Cincinnati, Ohio 45237

D. Salvation Today: A Personal Statement

M. M. Thomas

The major address at the Bangkok conference was evidence of how each person can and does interpret the saving act of God in Christ in light of his own need for and experience of salvation. It was equally witness to the commonality, with allowances for personal and cultural differences, of our experience of salvation in the church; for although the statement came from India it speaks to us all. It is included here, in a somewhat abridged form, in the belief that it will repay careful study, not least in its discussion of the meaning of a word that modern man finds increasingly hard to understand, the word spiritual.

Dr. M. M. Thomas, who is chairman of the Central Committee of the World Council of Churches, is a layman, a member of the Mar Thoma Syrian Church of Malabar, South India. He is director of the Christian Institute for the Study of Religion and Society, Bangalore.

I find my task this morning most difficult. Already, before coming here, we have waded through a mass of personal and group statements which express the search for salvation and its experience by people in a variety of situations, as well as evaluations of these from various perspectives. We have had studies on the biblical meaning of salvation; we have had several summaries of findings from Christian study groups in different parts of the world.

All this is so comprehensive that I have wondered what contribution I could make to the ongoing discussion which was not merely a repetition of some of the ideas already canvassed. Therefore, I have decided to speak from within my own situation, the Indian situation, and more particularly the situation of the Director of a Christian Institute engaged in explicating the gospel of Christ within and in relation to the Indian situation, and to articulate my own personal understanding of the meaning of human salvation offered in Jesus Christ. If I don't make sense, or make only partial sense, it will be because of the particularist situational and personal approach I am taking.

In 1956, when the National Christian Council of India and the Christian Institute for the Study of Society together launched the Study of Rapid Social Change in India, Dr. John Mathai, who was for some time Minister for Finance in Nehru's Government and was at that time head of the State Bank of India, gave the inaugural address. He spoke on the new pattern for the developed and just society which India was seeking to build. He concluded his talk by giving, as a Christian, his own vision of India's future, relating it to the picture we have in the final part of Psalm 144. He said, "In broad idealistic terms, allowing for the fact that the psalmist lived in a pastoral and primitive agricultural society and we live in a mainly industrial society, there is a great deal in common between the picture he paints in the 144th Psalm and the society we are trying to evolve:

> That our sons may grow up as the young plants and that our daughters may be as the polished corners of the Temple
>
> That our garners may be full and plenteous with all manner of store;
>
> That our sheep may bring forth thousands and ten thousands in our streets; that our oxen may be strong to labour;
>
> That there be no leading into captivity,
>
> And no complaining in our streets,
>
> Happy are the people that are in such a state,
>
> Blessed are the people who have the Lord for their God.

That was the first time that Psalm 144 came alive for me, as expressing the situation of a developing nation like India and voicing the aspirations and expectations of its people for a richer and fuller human life. The dynamism and the struggle, the hope and the despair in the situation are created by these aspirations, and the pursuit of what the psalmist calls happiness. He includes four elements in this prayer: first, health of body and beauty of form for youth;

second, the development of material abundance; third, security from aggression and peace; and fourth, social justice.

Material and Spiritual

The secular pursuit of happiness—peoples seeking a richer and fuller realization of the potentialities of their humanity through the building of a new society which will provide health and plenty, peace and justice—is the context within which I must speak of spiritual salvation. This is precisely what the Psalmist does. For, after picturing the society of his dreams, he says:

Happy the people to whom such blessings fall!
Happy the people whose God is the Lord!

The question is whether there is a vital relation between the two—between the happiness which the people realize through building a new and more human society and the happiness which they realize through acknowledging the Lord as God.

Spirituality

Here we enter a discussion of the meaning of the word *spiritual* as it pertains to man as a spiritual being. Man belongs to the animal species and is involved in the process and needs of organic nature, but what distinguishes man from animal is the knowledge he has that he is so involved, and his awareness of a self which, while involved in nature, also transcends it. It is this self-transcendence which constitutes the spiritual freedom and personal being of man. It does not at any time deny his involvement in the processes of animal nature and its needs, e.g. hunger or sex, but gives this a spiritual quality, for the involvement now takes place not within the realm of necessity but within a structure of meaning and sacredness which the self in the freedom of its self-transcendence chooses. Therefore, the involvement becomes for man a responsible act of spiritual self-realization.

Human spirituality, one might say, is the way in which man, in the freedom of his self-transcendence, seeks a structure of ultimate meaning and sacredness within which he can fulfil or realise himself in and through his involvement in the bodily, the material, and the social realities and relations of his life on earth. This means of course that if the structure of meaning and sacredness which men choose is false, a false spirituality results, and instead of self-fulfillment, there is self-disintegration. As Dr. Mathew P. John wrote: "Freudians have said that most, if not all, human actions are coloured by sex broadly defined. We may reverse the statement and say that in man the whole of sexuality is conditioned by humanity, that is, involved with questions of spirit, freedom and sacredness. Nothing that man does can be dissociated from his spirit. Man is not such a combination of spirit and body that certain actions can be considered as exclusively belonging to the body and having no reference to the spirit. In all action man acts in his wholeness, and each action may be an exercise of his freedom." (*Changing Pattern of Family in India*, CISRS, p. 66: p. 183). Human spirituality undergirds all human strivings for health and sex and development and justice. The only question is whether it is a true or false spirituality, that is whether the structure of ultimate meaning and sacredness to which it is committed is the meaning and sacredness which is truly ultimate, i.e. of God, or simply created by men in their self-centeredness and rejection of God, and therefore idolatrous.

I have often quoted Nicholas Berdyaev's statement which says that while the problem of my own bread is a material question, the problem of my neighbour's bread is a spiritual one, and that therefore economics is shot through with human spirituality. The psalmist envisages for his people bodily health and material wealth, security from aggression and social justice. He is, however, concerned with these good things as an expression of a certain spiritual relation between the people and God. That is to say, when they are recognized and received as blessings promised by God to his people in his covenant with them, which provides the structure of meaning for their lives, and as means to acknowledge God as the ultimate source of sacredness, then they become witnesses to God and to his salvation of his people.

Similarly, the primary concern of the Christian mission is also with the salvation of human spirituality, with man's right choices in the realm of self-transcendence, and with structure of ultimate meaning and sacredness.

Herein lies the mission of the church: it is to participate in the movements of human liberation in our time in such a way as to witness to Jesus Christ as the Source, the Judge, and the Redeemer of the human spirituality and its orientation as it is at work in these movements, and therefore as the Saviour of Man today.

Let me acknowledge that the redemption of human spirituality from idolatrous realms of meaning and sacredness has been the primary concern of Christian mission in the past; only it was seen in relation to the spirituality and the structures of meaning or sacredness behind the traditional societies. To continue to speak from within the Indian context, Christian missions have preached to the tribal people and villagers the deliverance of the human spirit from the domination of "the elemental spirits of the universe" peopling the sun, moon and stars, mountains, trees and rocks, and from fatalism of poverty; it has sought to shift sacredness from the cow and other animals to the human person; it has grappled with the spiritual demon behind the caste-system, and challenged communities with the reality of the eucharistic fellowship which transcends castes; it has broken the spiritual halo around the idolatrous asceticism which tended to consider abstinence in matters of food and sex as an instrument of salvation. The prophetic tradition helped to bring about the shift from ceremonial purity to righteousness in historical existence. In fact, the gospel that preached deliverance from those aspects of traditional spirituality which sanctioned the oppressive features of traditional religious and social structures contributed, in no small measure, to the reform of the spirit of Hinduism and the social awakening in India, as well as to the emergence of secular social values and ideologies.

And, if today the people of India are committed to strive for the new society as defined by Dr. John Mathai, it is due, in part as least, to the transformation of traditional spirituality made possible by the impact of the gospel of Christ, not only as presented by Christian missions but also as mediated, first through Western culture and later through the Indian cultural renaissance. The spiritual creativity behind today's revolutionary search for a society which harnesses nature through science and technology for human welfare, eliminates poverty and oppression, opens the door of participation in power structures to hitherto submerged groups, and moves towards a fraternity of free and equal persons has its source, in part at least, in Christ's salvation of the human spirit. One could speak of it as a new stage in God's process of creation.

Creation and Fall

But every new stage in creation has its fall; and every creativity in turning to false realms of meaning and sacredness becomes self-destructive and betrays the human liberation which it seeks and which is promised by Christ. The oppressive traditional order then gives place not to a new discipline of personal and social responsibility but to chaos and to self-seeking. Affluence is sought as the be-all and end-all of life and the finer social values are sacrificed.

The conquest of nature, carried to its extreme, destroys the sense of stewardship of nature and man's harmony with it. The green revolution and industrial development, which science and technology make possible, instead of increasing the welfare of all, serve to strengthen the forces of exploitation and to increase the gulf between the rich and the poor.

Revolutions for justice get lost in the fury of self-righteousness; they devour their own offspring and become sources of new oppression. Secularization, which delivers men from superstitions and oppressive religious institutions and dogmatism, succumbs to the institutionalism and dogmatism of self-sufficient secularism and self-redemptive historicism. Alienated from God in the structure of our spirit and in the resultant fear of ultimate disintegration, we make frantic efforts to achieve self-redemption by creating new religious and salvationist ideologies, only to see our idealism crumbling to the ground, leaving in its wake frustration and disintegration. This is the same old vicious circle of law, sin and death and we are today more conscious of its reality and its power than in any previous period.

It is precisely at this point that the victory of the Cross is relevant. The mission of the church in this context is to be present within the creative liberation movements of our time which the gospel of Christ itself has helped to shape, and so participate in them as to be able to communicate the genuine gospel of liberation, which liberates men from the vicious circle of sin and alienation, law and self-righteousness, frustration and death and brings them to Christ's new humanity where there is forgiveness and reconciliation, grace and justification and renewal and eternal life.

It is this message that will liberate the liberation movements from the false spiritual structures of meaning based on idolatrous worship of schemes of self-redemption, and thus redeem their creative impulses from self-destructive tendencies, enabling them to achieve their inner rationale of human emancipation. Our message of Christ's salvation is ever the same; it is the call to men and nations to turn "from idols to serve a living God" who has "translated us from the domain of darkness into the kingdom of his dear Son" Jesus Christ, in whom we are delivered from the ultimate spiritual insecurities of the self and "made free to love." Today "idols" and "darkness" have a new character; and "love" too must have new implications.

My main thesis is finished. Since my context and perspective have been very personal and partial I have left many aspects of the question of the meaning of Christian salvation unanswered. But I wish to mention a few points before closing.

First, I have been indifferent to the, to my mind, fruitless debate between the advocates of individual salvation and social salvation. That debate always leaves me cold. My emphasis has been on the salvation of man; and everything of man, his individuality and his collectivity included, has roots in different levels of self-awareness, sense of spiritual freedom and responsibility, and the search for what I have called meaning and sacredness. Individuality is no doubt a very high watermark of spiritual awareness and creativity but it is a latecomer in social history. Patterns of spirituality and search for meaning and sacredness have however informed tribes, ethnic groups and other organized communities, what the Bible calls the "nations," even before the modern age of liberal individualism had emerged. The gospel is for the "nations," as well as for individuals.

Beyond History

Second, will the creative processes and the liberation movements in history ever be redeemed from idolatrous structures of meaning and saved by Christ to the extent that we can hope for a relatively high degree of human emancipation this side of the eschatological hope of the final salvation? The answer to this depends upon the depth of the response of faith.

One version of the "beyond history" and "after life" which is very current among Christians involved in political movements of liberation, is to say that divine forgiveness in Christ and the fellowship of forgiven sinners can be experienced only "beyond politics" and "after the power struggles" of politics between the oppressed and the oppressors. The politics of liberation are conceived entirely under "the law of natural necessity" either as inevitable class war or inevitable international war. I have no doubt necessities of sinful nature play their part in all power struggles and must be reckoned with by those concerned with politics of liberation. I am not so utopian as to deny the inevitability of accumulated sin in social history. But I do not think the message of divine forgiveness and the *koinonia* in Christ created by it can be relegated to a realm "beyond" or "after" politics. Just as in the case of individuals, in the case of classes, nations and races also, divine forgiveness and the community of forgiveness can and must break through sinful necessities, transform them and make the struggle more human.

Third, we are living at a time when we are deeply conscious of pluralism in the world—pluralism of human situations and needs, of varied religions and secular cultures, with different traditions of metaphysics, ideologies and world views, in terms of which Christians themselves seek to express their commitment to, and confession of, Christ. So much so any kind of a unity in the doctrine of Christ or of salvation in Christ, which has been the goal of traditional Christian churches, is to my mind impossible to conceive except in religious imperialistic terms.

What kind of a criterion of Christian faith can we lay down in a pluralistic age? Dr. Hans Küng when he visited India recently said, that the criterion of faith could be that the believer should in some form acknowledge the person of Jesus as "decisive for life," that is to say, to translate in my terms, decisive for the knowledge of ultimate reality and the realization of the ultimate meaning of life and its fulfilment here and hereafter.

Salvation and the Church

If the above is true, and salvation in Christ is conceded outside the church, what is the significance of the church? I have assumed the role of the church as the essential agent of mission. But what is the church? What are the essential marks of the self-identity of the church? How should it be structured to participate in the various religious and secular communities and in the creative processes and liberation movements so that it may promote its mission of salvation? This needs to be more fully explored. But let me just list a few fragmentary and rather unconnected ideas:

1. I am personally convinced that the gathering for the study of the Word and the celebration of the Eucharist is the center of the church's fellowship. But whether the fellowship should be a separate religious community among other religious communities, with most of the primary levels of social living of the believers confined to the Christian circle, and even with a Christian law governing their conduct and recognized by the state as it is today in many countries of Asia, and surely in India, is a moot question.

2. In a situation like India where Christian conversion has come to mean a transfer of allegiance from one culture and juridical community to another, rather than from idols to God, through Christ, and where baptism has become almost like the old circumcision, how can baptism regain its true meaning of spiritual conversion? Is it by considering baptism a condition of membership of the church or a privilege of membership?

3. My friend the late E. V. Mathew often raised the question whether it is not better, for the sake of the Christian mission, that the church form new sects with a prophetic vocation within the movements of cultural creativity and social liberation, rather than try to bring about one organized Church of India, which may only mean several small ghettos joining forces to form one large ghetto.

Here let me stop. I leave all unanswered questions for this conference of experts to tackle.

E. Salvation in Contemporary Experience: A Selection of Texts

How may we be saved? is a question that concerns the poet, the physician, the revolutionary as much as the pastor or priest.

Collected here are a number of selections from contemporary writing of all kinds. Each says something to the theme. Any attentive reader will find in his daily reading others equally rewarding in helping to understand what modern man is hoping for and where he finds it. If he is thoughtful, he may come to understand better how the salvation of God in Christ feeds the hunger of the contemporary crowds as Jesus did in Galilee.

SALVATION AND MY NEIGHBOR

A personal experience told to
Gail Maynard, Guatemala.

Before I accepted Christ I did many things. I studied to be a witch doctor, and worse than that I quarreled with my neighbor. I didn't have a clear title to the land I inherited from my father, and he tried to get my inheritance from me. I managed to straighten that matter out, but was so angry with my neighbor that I wanted to see him dead. I tried putting a curse on him myself but nothing happened. Then I went to a witch doctor who was supposed to have more power. He told me his curse would work in five minutes, but still nothing happened.

Another peddler who was a Christian urged me many times to give up my old ways and accept Christ. At first I wouldn't listen to him, but little by little I saw that he had peace and happiness where I was sad all the time, and so desperate sometimes I was ready to commit suicide. Finally I asked him what to do. He quoted to me Matthew 11:28 and urged me to accept Christ, and finally I did. I accepted Christ in May of 1966 and He changed my life completely. After that my wife, my mother, my sisters, brother and cousin came to know the Lord. We have made friends with the neighbor who used to be our enemy, and he acknowledges that the Gospel is good. We pray that he and his family may soon come to know the Lord and also our other neighbors, and my wife's family who are still very much opposed to the Gospel.

TO HEAR THE WIND, TO TASTE THE AIR

*A personal experience told
to Rod Barr, USA.*

In high school I wanted to experience more and more of life and sleep prevented my studying during the day and chasing at night. A friend suggested that pills might keep me awake during the day and I tried them. The pills worked until the day I collapsed in school. From that point on I was a drug addict to my classmates.

Leaving school in my junior year I married to escape from my home, that school and the small town where I lived. In a year my marriage foundered on my unwillingness to accept a drunken husband every week-end.

For a year after that I worked at various jobs, drifted into night clubs as a singer and dancer using pills to keep me going three and four days without sleep or food. Men found me a willing companion and I sank into a life of pills and sex.

During that year I met a man. This man seemed different from the others and we married. For a period of two years we tried to make a home for our son. I became interested in working with others who used pills and other drugs in a self destruction pattern, but my husband did not like me to have any interests outside the home.

Quarreling constantly, we seemed unable to find any of the love which had drawn us together. We separated and I fled. I fled into the world of drug use, actually drug abuse. I took my son to my parents and started running with one man after another. Festivals and drugs became a pattern of life for me. Always during this time I kept searching for what would make sense and found it in the experience of the minute, an experience which I called love.

One night in the midst of despair I sat down in a corner trying to make sense out of my life and finally turned to a friend and asked if I needed help. Without hesitation he said yes. I did not believe him and a few days later started running again. Then I watched as though on a trip my participation in the destruction of another person. And it burst upon me that I could run again or I could begin to make sense out of my life.

A minister put me in touch with professional help. And so began the slow search for reality for me and my son. None of this proceeded in a steady path. I ran again several times and still may run. For now I work, care for my son and search within me for meaning. The search within means seeking professional help to explore why I lived and want to live running. The search within means the discovery that in all the communities I know Christians keep trying in the midst of falling.

For me life is a reflection of joy. To hear the wind, to taste the air, to run in the sunshine, to play with my son and to work becomes ways that I will be saved. What must I do to be saved? I must learn me, discover values which fit me—some of which I rejected. And I need to live in community where people can care for one another.

A LETTER TO GOD

Nestor Paz Zamora ("Francisco") was one of the university students who were involved in the armed conflict in Bolivia, beginning in July 1970. He understood his guerilla commitment as an evangelical imperative. His "campaign diary" is less a record of combat action than a meditation, a continual conversation with God. He was killed in guerilla action on October 8, 1970. (IDOC—International 10/4, 1971)

Dear Lord,

It has been a long time since I wrote to you. Today I feel a real need for you and your presence, perhaps because of the nearness of death or the relative failure of the struggle. You know that I have tried to be faithful to you—always and by all means—consistent with my whole being. That is why I am here. I understand love as the urgency of helping to solve the problems of the "other person"—in whom you are present.

I left what I had and came here. Perhaps today is my (Maundy) Thursday and tonight my (Good) Friday. Because I love you I surrender everything I am into your hands, without limit. What hurts me is the thought of leaving those I most love—Cecy and my family—and perhaps not being here to participate in the triumph of the people—their liberation.

We are a group full of true, "Christian" humanity, and I think we will change the course of history. The thought of this comforts me. I love you and I give you myself and ourselves, completely, because you are my Father. No one's death is meaningless if his life has been charged with significance; and I believe this has been true of us, here.

Ciao, Lord! Perhaps until that heaven of yours, that new world we desire so much!

SALVATION AND HUMANIZATION

M. M. Thomas is Director of the Christian Institute for the Study of Religion and Society, Bangalore, India. This passage is taken from International Review of Mission, *January, 1971, pp. 34-5.*

In spite of these obstacles, however, the outcastes, the poor and the orphans saw the Christian faith as the source of a new humanizing influence and the foundation of a human community. Where conversion was genuine, whether of individuals or groups, the converts saw Salvation in Christ not only in terms of individual salvation or heaven after death, but also as the spiritual source of a new community on earth in which their human dignity and status were recognized. It was the promise of humanization inherent in the Gospel of salvation that led to the influx of the oppressed into the Church.

It was the same promise in Christ's Salvation of a richer and fuller human life for all men in society and of a new community of freedom and love that attracted some of the intellectuals of the privileged classes of India and brought them to acknowledge Christ as their Lord and God. The young C. F. Andrews, when he joined St. Stephen's College, Delhi as a missionary, interviewed many "leading Indian converts" and enquired of them "the special causes which had led them to become Christians". Here is what Andrews found:

One after another omitted that cause which I should have imagined to be primary—namely the longing for personal salvation. Some told me that it was the moral perfection of Christ's character, especially as seen in the Sermon on the Mount—the attraction of the *Christian moral standard.* Many replied that it was the freedom of the Christian life compared with the bondage of caste—the attraction of the *Christian brotherhood.* Others stated that it was the thought of Christ uniting all the divided races and peoples of India into one—the ideal of the *Christian Church*. But I found no case in which the individual's own need was the sole or even primary factor.

He adds:

I do not imply by this that the sense of individual need of salvation is absent or that this experience is necessarily typical. But in such instances as these, the purely personal aspects develop later. The community is the primary concern.

In other words, it is the personal appeal of the Gospel of the Crucified and Risen Christ seen as the foundation of Christian fellowship and the larger secular brotherhood that made them decide for Christ as the bearer of ultimate destiny.

MODELS OF HEALTH AND SALVATION

R. Lambourne, late professor of psychiatry in the University of Birmingham, was the author of Community, Church and Healing. *A study of some of the corporate aspects of the church's ministry to the sick. London: Darton, Longman and Todd, 1963.*

I was in the USA when some medical students with a social conscience revolted because they were appalled at working and being taught in one of the most advanced medical centres in the world, whilst they were literally within a stone's throw of the downtown area where people weren't getting any medical care. The medical students refused to be taught anymore and went out and began giving health care. Although this health care was, in terms of the hospital, less skilled, it was in fact more excellent in terms of its ultimate result of the relief of suffering than that which the hospital was giving.

Again, there was a man who went to a famous pediatric hospital in Africa which had been in existence for fifty years and the people and church were proud of it, for every child who came to the hospital received the best treatment. Then this new paediatrician came, no more devoted nor less a Christian than the previous one; but he looked at the infant mortality rate in the area served by the hospital and discovered that it hadn't altered at all over the years. It was about 282 per 1000 and would stay that high as long as excellent medicine was practised in the hospital! It wasn't hard for him to discover that the children were dying of three diseases, A, B, and C. One was malaria. If you can talk to the people, feel the spleen and give a tablet R, by and large you can put the matter right. Another disease was some kind of dysentery: by talking to the people, having a rough look at the stool, if you can persuade the child's mother to give tablet S it will cure the disease in most cases. The third disease, I think, was sores; and again it was not very difficult to solve the problem, provided you are willing to make mistakes in diagnosis, but you have to be willing to make mistakes. This paediatrician had been taught back home that individual excellence of diagnosis is the mark of a doctor, but he had to produce, first in himself and then in other doctors a new professional style and a new personal excellence suitable to the job required of them. Therefore, he took a few girls out of the local mission school, aged about fifteen, taught them and sent them into the villages. They made an enormous number of mistakes, some of them disastrous from the traditional medical point of view. He was fortunate there wasn't a legal system where they could sue for wrong diagnosis. But in five years' time the infant mortality dropped to 78 per 1000. Now what was killing all those children before? A sacred, stereotyped view of excellence! That is, a graven image of excellence, tempting us to idolatry.

RELIGION AND THE POST-REVOLUTIONARY GENERATION

A. E. Levitin-Krasnov is one of the most important spokesmen for the independent critical movements within the Russian Orthodox Church. Most of his writings appear in Russia not in print but in typed copies passed from hand to hand. In this letter to Pope Paul VI he describes the intellectual and religious renewal movement in Russia in which the laity are playing a leading role.

Modern youth holds a quite exceptional place in the matter of religion—the third post-revolutionary generation. As a rule these are persons who have no conception of religion, having received a clearly expressed anti-religious up-bringing. Although it may appear strange, this has not only a negative but also a positive side for the promotion of religion. The positive is this, that modern youth simply does not know the negative aspects of pre-revolutionary Orthodoxy, which widely led to hatred and bitterness on the part of the people. They do not remember the times when religion was obligatory, when the Church was an official institution, a support for Tsarism. They do not remember the pre-revolutionary clergy, an inherited caste, in which as a consequence there were many persons ordained to church service without any inner calling, by inertia, and looking upon their responsibilities with purely professional unconcern. Our youth is often without religion, frequently infected with anti-religious prejudices, as a result of which they look upon religion as the root of darkness and ignorance. Among them, however, one does not find the anti-religious fanaticism and animosity of their grandfathers. . . . The average representative of the younger generation approaches religion with mixed feelings of incredulity and interest. . . .

In most cases the process of conversion to Christ takes place instinctively, and a special role in it belongs to the laity. The apostolate of the laity, of which so much was said at the last Vatican Council, and on which so much is now written in the West, has been an actuality here with us in Russia for some years. In the great majority of cases of conversion, the role of the priest is only to conduct the sacrament of baptism, whereas conversion itself and catechization, i.e. preparation for baptism, often is done apart from the clergy.

Young people newly coming to the Church are usually filled with the desire to proselytize, and they in turn lead other boys and girls, their companions and friends, to God.

THE STORY OF ANTONIO JOSE DOS SANTOS

This story was recorded by D. E. Curry during his anthropological research on the development of Protestant groups in the interior of Brazil. Antonio told how he was converted and received a call to go and preach the Gospel. He then set out on a troublesome journey, never being permitted to stay more than a few months at any one place.

Once more I had to move on, so I returned to Sergipe and Campo Nôvo where my wife and children were and preached the Gospel there. The owner of the farm and his entire family were converted and I started a small congregation. After eight days the people from Santa Brigida who had been converted began moving in over the thirty kilometers of trail between the two places. These people fled from Santa Brigida by night because of fear of the Captain of Police, José Rufino, and other people in the town. They came in groups of twenty-five at a time and within a few days there were about thirty families at Campo Nôvo, which amounted to about one hundred and fifty persons. We stayed there together for four years and eight months. . . .

Now the owner of Campo Nôvo farm who had been converted had a son who had been absent for some years in the city of Sao Paulo. One day he came home and found all of those *crentes* farming on his father's property and he began immediately to agitate to have his father send us away upon the pretext we would eventually take the land entirely away from his father and the heirs. Really, though, what he wanted was the improvements we had put on the land in those years of hard work: thirteen good houses, five *acudas* (reservoirs for water) and a large number of *tarefas* (unit of land measure equal to three-fourths of an acre in Sergipe) of rice, beans, and cotton. His father finally agreed to his demands and I went to the authorities of the *municipio* asking them to try and intercede for us at least some sort of partial payment for all we had to leave behind. On 27 May 1958 sixty crentes followed me leaving behind everything and we all traveled forty-five kilometers to another fazenda named Belo Horizonte. . . .

The *fazendeiro* of Belo Horizonte was named Agostinho Barbosa dos Anjos and he took all of us in, offering us land. He told us he would sell the land to us so we would never be chased again. But we did not have any money with which to pay. He said that it did not matter. I was to stay and work with the people and pay him as we could. After nine months at Belo Horizonte he gave us a written title by means of which I and all the people became registered owners of 2,300 tarefas. We had to work three years more in order to pay for it in full but after this we were free to move onto the property and build our homes on it. This is the settlement we have built, and are still building, and we call it Fazenda Nova Vida (New Life Farm). To the thirty families who moved here with me I appointed a piece of ground, all that they were able to work, and gave them a property document for it. Each family received land according to its size and the number of hands it was able to put to work. The church we have built we call the Evangelho de Paz (Good Tidings of Peace). The public authorities of the municipio of Poço Redondo, in which Belo Horizonte was located at the time we came, refused to have anything to do with us up to and including the state authorities until this very day. On September 1963, our church joined the Assembly of God *igreja-mãe* of Aracajú.

MEDITATIONS ON SALVATION FROM BANGKOK

Members of one group at the Bangkok Conference undertook to write down their own deeply felt prayers. From those that were collected the following especially may be of help to others.

A PRAYER OF PRAISE

We praise You, God our Father,
   for the wild richness of your creation
   for the uniqueness of each person,
   for the creativity, sustaining and renewing our cultures,
   for your faithfulness towards your people.

We praise You, Jesus our Lord,
   for your constant meddling in our affairs,
   for your identification with the poor,
   for your sacrifice for all men on the cross,
   for revealing the true man to all people.

We praise You, God the Spirit,
   for your inspiration of life,
   for your translation of the anguish of creation,
   for your insistence to draw us always to Christ,
   for the infusion of unrest among man,
   for your patient preparation of the fulfilment of history.

We praise You, blessed Trinity,
   for not doing to us according to our sins,
   for continuing your love to all that lives,
   for continuing your disturbing call to repentance,
   for continuing life on earth.

A PRAYER OF INTERCESSION

For people caught in exploitation,
neglected by systems, raped by ideologies,
caught between machines, shrivelled up by loneliness,
hardened by their convictions, deaf for surprises,
blind for suffering, crippled by unfreedom,
we pray: Out of the depths we cry unto Thee, O Lord!
For Christ's Church on earth,
confused about its message, uncertain about its role,
divided in many ways, polarized between different understandings,
unimaginative in its proclamation, undisciplined in its fellowship,
we pray: Out of the depths we cry unto Thee, O Lord!
For ourselves in this Conference,
overwhelmed by our impressions, torn apart by prejudice,
often in doubt, plagued by frustrations,
struggling for honesty, for understanding of each other,
crying for love, searching for justice,
we pray: Out of the depths we cry unto Thee, O Lord!

A LITANY

God of Moses, saved in the river;
God of Israel, freed from Egypt, freed from the desert;
God of the slain Lamb, powerless Lion of Judea;
God of Brazil, of the millions exploited by the black magic of growth;
God of Mexico, of the ambivalence of the revolution;
God of New York, of disappointment and of new life;
God of the theologians, deceived by the wind of doctrine;
God of the bureaucrats, nervously searching for new programs;
God of Africa, of a growing church in a land of exploitation;
God of the religious people, caught in the projection of their own mind;
God of the conservatives, of the burning desire to save souls;
God of the liberals, dreaming of reform;
God of the radicals, dreaming of revolution;
God of the artists, creativity of man;

God of the technocrats, enslaved to the power they hold;
God of the exploiters, love of power;
God of the Christians, between faith and unfaith;
God of those who have never heard of Jesus Christ;
God of those who have heard of Christ but only see his people;
God of us—God of all men,
surprise us anew with your faithfulness, save us today!

A LITANY OF PRAISE AND PRAYER

O God,
You have called us out of death, We praise you!
    Send us back with the bread of life, We pray you!
You have turned us around, We praise you!
    Keep us faithful, We pray you!
You have begun a good work, We praise you!
    Complete your salvation in us, We pray you!
You have made us a chosen people, We praise you!
    Make us one with all people, We pray you!
You have taught us your law, We praise you!
    Change us by the Spirit's power, We pray you!
You have sent your Son in one place and time, We praise you!
    Be present in every time and place, We pray you!
Your kingdom has come in his salvation, We praise you!
    Let it come always among us, We pray you!

LORD, TEACH US SILENCE

Lord, teach us the silence of humility
   the silence of wisdom
   the silence of love
   the silence that speaks without words
   the silence of faith.
Lord, teach us to silence our own hearts and minds
   that we may listen to the movement of the Holy Spirit
   within us and sense the depths which are God.